Developing
Essential Understanding
of
Ratios, Proportions, *and* Proportional Reasoning

for Teaching Mathematics *in*
Grades 6–8

Joanne Lobato
San Diego State University
San Diego, California

Amy B. Ellis
University of Wisconsin–Madison
Madison, Wisconsin

Randall I. Charles
Volume Editor
Carmel, California

Rose Mary Zbiek
Series Editor
The Pennsylvania State University
University Park, Pennsylvania

NATIONAL COUNCIL OF
TEACHERS OF MATHEMATICS

Copyright © 2010 by
The National Council of Teachers of Mathematics, Inc.
1906 Association Drive, Reston, VA 20191-1502
(703) 620-9840; (800) 235-7566; www.nctm.org
All rights reserved
Fifth printing 2016

Library of Congress Cataloging-in-Publication Data

Lobato, Joanne (Joanne Elizabeth)
  Developing essential understanding of ratios, proportions, and
proportional reasoning for teaching mathematics in grades 6-8 / Joanne
Lobato, Amy B. Ellis ; Randall I. Charles, volume editor ; Rose Mary
Zbiek, series editor.
      p. cm.
  "Essential understanding series"--Pref.
  Includes bibliographical references.
  ISBN 978-0-87353-622-6
  1. Mathematics--Study and teaching (Middle school)--Standards--United
States. 2. Middle school education--Curricula--Standards--United
States. 3. Curriculum planning--Standards--United States. I. Ellis,
Amy B. II. Charles, Randall I. (Randall Inners), 1949- III. Title.
  QA135.6.L63 2010
  372.7--dc22
                                   2010005422

The National Council of Teachers of Mathematics is the public voice of mathematics education, supporting teachers to ensure equitable mathematics learning of the highest quality for all students through vision, leadership, professional development, and research.

Printed in the United States of America

Contents

Foreword

Teaching mathematics in prekindergarten–grade 12 requires a special understanding of mathematics. Effective teachers of mathematics think about and beyond the content that they teach, seeking explanations and making connections to other topics, both inside and outside mathematics. Students meet curriculum and achievement expectations when they work with teachers who know what mathematics is important for each topic that they teach.

The National Council of Teachers of Mathematics (NCTM) presents the Essential Understanding Series in tandem with a call to focus the school mathematics curriculum in the spirit of *Curriculum Focal Points for Prekindergarten through Grade 8 Mathematics: A Quest for Coherence*, published in 2006, and *Focus in High School Mathematics: Reasoning and Sense Making,* released in 2009. The Essential Understanding books are a resource for individual teachers and groups of colleagues interested in engaging in mathematical thinking to enrich and extend their own knowledge of particular mathematics topics in ways that benefit their work with students. The topic of each book is an area of mathematics that is difficult for students to learn, challenging to teach, and critical for students' success as learners and in their future lives and careers.

Drawing on their experiences as teachers, researchers, and mathematicians, the authors have identified the big ideas that are at the heart of each book's topic. A set of essential understandings— mathematical points that capture the essence of the topic—fleshes out each big idea. Taken collectively, the big ideas and essential understandings give a view of a mathematics that is focused, connected, and useful to teachers. Links to topics that students encounter earlier and later in school mathematics and to instruction and assessment practices illustrate the relevance and importance of a teacher's essential understanding of mathematics.

On behalf of the Board of Directors, I offer sincere thanks and appreciation to everyone who has helped to make this series possible. I extend special thanks to Rose Mary Zbiek for her leadership as series editor. I join the Essential Understanding project team in welcoming you to these books and in wishing you many years of continued enjoyment of learning and teaching mathematics.

Henry Kepner
President, 2008–2010
National Council of Teachers of Mathematics

Preface

From prekindergarten through grade 12, the school mathematics curriculum includes important topics that are pivotal in students' development. Students who understand these ideas cross smoothly into new mathematical terrain and continue moving forward with assurance.

However, many of these topics have traditionally been challenging to teach as well as learn, and they often prove to be barriers rather than gateways to students' progress. Students who fail to get a solid grounding in them frequently lose momentum and struggle in subsequent work in mathematics and related disciplines.

The Essential Understanding Series identifies such topics at all levels. Teachers who engage students in these topics play critical roles in students' mathematical achievement. Each volume in the series invites teachers who aim to be not just proficient but outstanding in the classroom—teachers like you—to enrich their understanding of one or more of these topics to ensure students' continued development in mathematics.

How much do you need to know?

To teach these challenging topics effectively, you must draw on a mathematical understanding that is both broad and deep. The challenge is to know considerably more about the topic than you expect your students to know and learn.

Why does your knowledge need to be so extensive? Why must it go above and beyond what you need to teach and your students need to learn? The answer to this question has many parts.

To plan successful learning experiences, you need to understand different models and representations and, in some cases, emerging technologies as you evaluate curriculum materials and create lessons. As you choose and implement learning tasks, you need to know what to emphasize and why those ideas are mathematically important.

While engaging your students in lessons, you must anticipate their perplexities, help them avoid known pitfalls, and recognize and dispel misconceptions. You need to capitalize on unexpected classroom opportunities to make connections among mathematical ideas. If assessment shows that students have not understood the material adequately, you need to know how to address weaknesses that you have identified in their understanding. Your understanding must be sufficiently versatile to allow you to represent the mathematics in different ways to students who don't understand it the first time. In addition, you need to know where the topic fits in the full span of the mathematics curriculum. You must understand where your students are coming from in their thinking and where they are heading mathematically in the months and years to come.

Accomplishing these tasks in mathematically sound ways is a tall order. A rich understanding of the mathematics supports the varied work of teaching as you guide your students and keep their learning on track.

How can the Essential Understanding Series help?

The Essential Understanding books offer you an opportunity to delve into the mathematics that you teach and reinforce your content knowledge. They do not include materials for you to use directly with your students, nor do they discuss classroom management, teaching styles, or assessment techniques. Instead, these books focus squarely on issues of mathematical content—the ideas and understanding that you must bring to your preparation, in-class instruction, one-on-one interactions with students, and assessment.

How do the authors approach the topics?

For each topic, the authors identify "big ideas" and "essential understandings." The big ideas are mathematical statements of overarching concepts that are central to a mathematical topic and link numerous smaller mathematical ideas into coherent wholes. The books call the smaller, more concrete ideas that are associated with each big idea *essential understandings*. They capture aspects of the corresponding big idea and provide evidence of its richness.

The big ideas have tremendous value in mathematics. You can gain an appreciation of the power and worth of these densely packed statements through persistent work with the interrelated essential understandings. Grasping these multiple smaller concepts and through them gaining access to the big ideas can greatly increase your intellectual assets and classroom possibilities.

In your work with mathematical ideas in your role as a teacher, you have probably observed that the essential understandings are often at the heart of the understanding that you need for presenting one of these challenging topics to students. Knowing these ideas very well is critical because they are the mathematical pieces that connect to form each big idea.

How are the books organized?

Every book in the Essential Understanding Series has the same structure:

- The introduction gives an overview, explaining the reasons for the selection of the particular topic and highlighting some of the differences between what teachers and students need to know about it.

- Chapter 1 is the heart of the book, identifying and examining the big ideas and related essential understandings.

Big ideas and essential understandings are identified by icons in the books.

marks a big idea,

and

marks an essential understanding.

- Chapter 2 reconsiders the ideas discussed in chapter 1 in light of their connections with mathematical ideas within the grade band and with other mathematics that students have encountered earlier or will encounter later in their study of mathematics.

- Chapter 3 wraps up the discussion by considering the challenges that students often face in grasping the necessary concepts related to the topic under discussion. It analyzes the development of their thinking and offers guidance for presenting ideas to them and assessing their understanding.

The discussion of big ideas and essential understandings in chapter 1 is interspersed with questions labeled "Reflect." It is important to pause in your reading to think about these on your own or discuss them with your colleagues. By engaging with the material in this way, you can make the experience of reading the book participatory, interactive, and dynamic.

Reflect questions can also serve as topics of conversation among local groups of teachers or teachers connected electronically in school districts or even between states. Thus, the Reflect items can extend the possibilities for using the books as tools for formal or informal experiences for in-service and preservice teachers, individually or in groups, in or beyond college or university classes.

A new perspective

The Essential Understanding Series thus is intended to support you in gaining a deep and broad understanding of mathematics that can benefit your students in many ways. Considering connections between the mathematics under discussion and other mathematics that students encounter earlier and later in the curriculum gives the books unusual depth as well as insight into vertical articulation in school mathematics.

The series appears against the backdrop of *Principles and Standards for School Mathematics* (NCTM 2000), *Curriculum Focal Points for Prekindergarten through Grade 8 Mathematics: A Quest for Coherence* (NCTM 2006), *Focus in High School Mathematics: Reasoning and Sense Making* (NCTM 2009), and the Navigations Series (NCTM 2001–2009). The new books play an important role, supporting the work of these publications by offering content-based professional development.

The other publications, in turn, can flesh out and enrich the new books. After reading this book, for example, you might select hands-on, Standards-based activities from the Navigations books for your students to use to gain insights into the topics that the Essential Understanding books discuss. If you are teaching students in prekindergarten through grade 8, you might apply your deeper understanding as you present material related to the three focal points that *Curriculum Focal Points* identifies for instruction at your students' level. Or if you are teaching students in grades 9–12, you might use your understanding to enrich the ways in which you can engage students in mathematical reasoning and sense making as presented in *Focus in High School Mathematics*.

An enriched understanding can give you a fresh perspective and infuse new energy into your teaching. We hope that the understanding that you acquire from reading the book will support your efforts as you help your students grasp the ideas that will ensure their mathematical success.

The authors of the present volume would like to thank the following individuals who reviewed an earlier version of the book: Steven Benson, Rick Billstein, Glenda Lappan, and Barbara Zorin. Their careful reading and willingness to share their reactions were greatly appreciated.

Introduction

This book focuses on ideas about ratios, proportions, and proportional reasoning. These are ideas that you need to understand thoroughly and be able to use flexibly to be highly effective in your teaching of mathematics in grades 6–8. The book discusses many mathematical ideas that are common in middle school curricula, and it assumes that you have had a variety of mathematics experiences that have motivated you to delve into—and move beyond—the mathematics that you expect your students to learn.

The book is designed to engage you with these ideas, helping you to develop an understanding that will guide you in planning and implementing lessons and assessing your students' learning in ways that reflect the full complexity of ratios and proportional relationships. A deep, rich understanding of these relationships will enable you to communicate their influence and scope to your students, showing them how these ideas permeate the mathematics that they have encountered—and will continue to encounter—throughout their school mathematics experiences.

The understanding of ratios, proportions, and proportional reasoning that you gain from this focused study thus supports the vision of *Principles and Standards for School Mathematics* (NCTM 2000): "Imagine a classroom, a school, or a school district where all students have access to high-quality, engaging mathematics instruction" (p. 3). This vision depends on classroom teachers who "are continually growing as professionals" (p. 3) and routinely engage their students in meaningful experiences that help them learn mathematics with understanding.

Why Ratios, Proportions, and Proportional Reasoning?

Like the topics of all the volumes in NCTM's Essential Understanding Series, ratios, proportions, and proportional reasoning compose a major area of school mathematics that is crucial for students to learn but challenging for teachers to teach. Students in grades 6–8 need to understand proportionality well if they are to succeed in these grades and in their subsequent mathematics experiences. Learners often struggle with ideas about ratio and proportion. What is the relationship between ratios and fractions, for example? Many students mistakenly believe that they are identical. The importance of ratios, proportions, and proportional reasoning and the challenge of understanding them well make them essential for teachers of mathematics in grades 6–8 to understand extremely well themselves.

Your work as a middle school teacher of mathematics calls for a solid understanding of the mathematics that you—and your school, your district, and your state curriculum—expect your students to learn about ratios, proportions, and proportional reasoning. Your work also requires you to know how this mathematics relates to other mathematical ideas that your students will encounter in the lesson at hand, the current school year, and beyond. Rich mathematical understanding guides teachers' decisions in much of their work, such as choosing tasks for a lesson, posing questions, selecting materials, ordering topics and ideas over time, assessing the quality of students' work, and devising ways to challenge and support their thinking.

Understanding Ratios, Proportions, and Proportional Reasoning

Teachers teach mathematics because they want others to understand it in ways that will contribute to success and satisfaction in school, work, and life. Helping your middle school students develop a robust and lasting understanding of ratios, proportions, and proportional reasoning requires that you understand this mathematics deeply. But what does this mean?

It is easy to think that understanding an area of mathematics, such as ratios and proportions, means knowing certain facts, being able to solve particular types of problems, and mastering relevant vocabulary. For example, for the middle school level, you are expected to know such facts as "a ratio can be written in different ways." You are expected to be skillful in solving problems that involve such activities as setting up and solving a proportion. Your mathematical vocabulary is assumed to include such terms as *ratio*, *proportion*, *proportionality*, and *rate*.

Obviously, facts, vocabulary, and techniques for solving certain types of problems are not all that you are expected to know about ratios, proportions, and proportional reasoning. In your ongoing work with students, you have undoubtedly discovered that you need to distinguish among different types of problems and know when particular strategies apply. For example, you must know the difference between relationships that are proportional and relationships that are not proportional. For proportional relationships, you need to understand what it means for ratios to be equivalent and different ways of generating equivalent ratios.

It is also easy to focus on a very long list of mathematical ideas that all teachers of mathematics in grades 6–8 are expected to know and teach about ratios and proportions. Curriculum developers often devise and publish such lists. However important the individual items might be, these lists cannot capture the essence of a rich understanding of the topic. Understanding this area deeply requires you not only to know important mathematical ideas but also to recognize how these ideas relate to one another. Your understanding continues to grow with experience and as a result of opportunities to embrace new ideas and find new connections among familiar ones.

Furthermore, your understanding of ratios, proportions, and proportional reasoning should transcend the content intended for your students. Some of the differences between what you need to know and what you expect them to learn are easy to point out. For instance, your understanding of the topic should include a grasp of the way in which ratios and proportions connect with linear functions—mathematics that students will encounter later but do not yet understand.

Other differences between the understanding that you need to have and the understanding that you expect your students to acquire are less obvious, but your experiences in the classroom have undoubtedly made you aware of them at some level. For example, how many times have you been grateful to have an understanding of ratios, proportions, and proportional reasoning that enables you to recognize the merit in a student's unanticipated mathematical question or claim? How many other times have you wondered whether you could be missing such an opportunity or failing to use it to full advantage because of a gap in your knowledge?

As you have almost certainly discovered, knowing and being able to do familiar mathematics are not enough when you're in the classroom. You also need to be able to identify and justify or refute novel claims. These claims and justifications might draw on ideas or techniques that are beyond the mathematical experiences of your students and current curricular expectations for them. For example, you need to be able to refute the often-asserted, erroneous claim that all ratios are fractions. At the same time, you should be able to illustrate conceptual relationships between fractions and ratios, as well as use fractional notation to express ratios.

Big Ideas and Essential Understandings

Thinking about the many particular ideas that are part of a rich understanding of ratios, proportions, and proportional reasoning can be an overwhelming task. Articulating all of those mathematical ideas and their connections would require many books. To choose which ideas to include in this book, the authors considered a critical question: What is *essential* for teachers of mathematics in grades 6–8 to know about ratios, proportions, and proportional reasoning to be effective in the classroom? To answer this question, the authors drew on a variety of resources, including personal experiences, the expertise of colleagues in mathematics and mathematics education, and the reactions of reviewers and professional development providers, as well as ideas from curricular materials and research on mathematics learning and teaching.

As a result, the mathematical content of this book focuses on essential knowledge for teachers about ratios, proportions, and proportional reasoning. In particular, chapter 1 is organized around one big idea related to this important area of mathematics. This big idea is supported by smaller, more specific mathematical ideas, which the book calls *essential understandings*. This book focuses on ten interconnected essential understandings that are related to the big idea. These ideas elaborate what you need to know for an understanding of ratios, proportions, and proportional reasoning. Gaining this understanding is an extremely valuable and useful accomplishment because ratios and proportions offer ways to think quantitatively about real-world phenomena.

Benefits for Teaching, Learning, and Assessing

An understanding of ratios, proportions, and proportional reasoning can help you implement the Teaching Principle enunciated in *Principles and Standards for School Mathematics*. This Principle sets a high standard for instruction: "Effective mathematics teaching requires understanding what students know and need to learn and then challenging and supporting them to learn it well" (NCTM 2000, p. 16). As in teaching about other critical topics in mathematics, teaching about ratios, proportions, and proportional reasoning requires knowledge that goes "beyond what most teachers experience in standard preservice mathematics courses" (p. 17).

Chapter 1 comes into play at this point, offering an overview of proportionality that is intended to be more focused and comprehensive than many discussions of the topic that you are likely to have encountered. This chapter enumerates, expands on, and gives examples of the big idea and essential understandings related to ratios, proportions, and proportional reasoning, with the goal of supplementing or reinforcing your understanding. Thus, chapter 1 aims to prepare you to implement the Teaching Principle fully as you provide the support and challenge that your students need for robust learning about proportionality.

Consolidating your understanding in this way also prepares you to implement the Learning Principle outlined in *Principles and Standards*: "Students must learn mathematics with understanding, actively building new knowledge from experience and prior knowledge" (NCTM 2000, p. 20). To support your efforts to help your students learn about ratios, proportions, and proportional reasoning in this way, chapter 2 builds on the understanding of the topic that chapter 1 communicates by pointing out specific ways in which the big idea and essential understandings connect with mathematics that students typically encounter earlier or later in school. This chapter supports the Learning Principle by emphasizing longitudinal connections in students' learning about proportionality.

For example, as their mathematical experiences expand, students gradually develop an understanding of the connections between proportionality and relationships that they can represent by equations of the form $y = ax$, together with an understanding of the connections between proportionality and relationships that they can represent by equations of the form $y = ax + b$.

The understanding that chapters 1 and 2 convey can strengthen another critical area of teaching. Chapter 3 addresses this area, building on the first two chapters to show how an understanding of ratios, proportions, and proportional reasoning can help you select and develop appropriate tasks, techniques, and tools for assessing your students' understanding of the topic. An ownership of the big idea and essential understandings related to proportionality, reinforced by an awareness of students' past and future experiences with the ideas, can help you ensure that assessment in your classroom supports the learning of significant mathematics.

Such assessment satisfies the first requirement of the Assessment Principle set out in *Principles and Standards* (NCTM 2000): "Assessment should support the learning of important mathematics and furnish useful information to both teachers and students" (p. 22). An understanding of ratios, proportions, and proportional reasoning can also help you satisfy the second requirement of the Assessment Principle, by enabling you to develop assessment tasks that give you specific information about what your students are thinking and what they understand. For instance, consider comparison problems and transformation problems. Comparison problems typically show students two ratios and ask them to determine whether the first ratio is greater than, less than, or equal to the second. Transformation problems give a ratio or two equivalent ratios and ask students either to change one or more quantities to change the ratio relationship or to determine how a given change in one or more quantities changes the relationship. Using a combination of these (and other) types of problems can give you insights about the range of strategies that students have developed and the ways in which they reason about quantities and relationships.

Ready to Begin

This introduction has painted the background, preparing you for the big idea and associated essential understandings related to proportionality that you will encounter and explore in chapter 1. Reading the chapters in the order in which they appear can be a very useful way to approach the book. Read chapter 1 in more than one sitting, allowing time for reflection. Absorb the ideas—both the big idea and the essential understandings—that contribute to an understanding of ratios, proportions, and proportional reasoning. Appreciate the connections among these ideas. Carry your new-found or reinforced understanding to chapter 2, which guides you in seeing how the ideas related to ratios, proportions, and proportional reasoning are connected to the mathematics that your students have encountered earlier or will encounter later in school. Then read about teaching, learning, and assessment issues in chapter 3.

Alternatively, you may want to take a look at chapter 3 before engaging with the mathematical ideas in chapters 1 and 2. Having the challenges of teaching, learning, and assessment issues clearly in mind, along with possible approaches to them, can give you a different perspective on the material in the earlier chapters.

No matter how you read the book, let it serve as a tool to expand your understanding, application, and enjoyment of ratios, proportions, and proportional reasoning.

Chapter 1

Ratios, Proportions, and Proportional Reasoning:
The Big Idea and Essential Understandings

A TYPICAL instructional unit or chapter on ratio and proportion shows students different ways to write ratios and then introduces a proportion as two equivalent ratios. Next, students usually encounter the cross-multiplication algorithm as a technique for solving a proportion. Does this customary development of ratio and proportion promote a deep understanding of these ideas? Consider an interview with a student named Bonita to think about what it means to reason proportionally.

Bonita was given a problem about a leaky faucet through which 6 ounces of water dripped in 8 minutes. She needed to figure out how much water dripped in 4 minutes. Bonita set up a proportion and used cross multiplication, as shown in figure 1.1, to arrive at a correct response of 3 ounces. Reflect 1.1 invites you to think about Bonita's work on the problem.

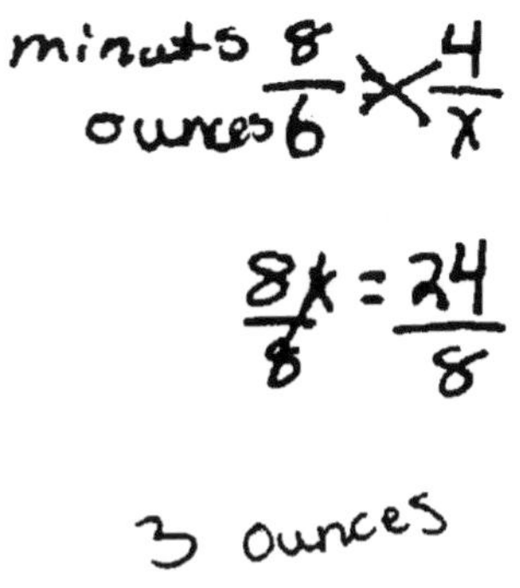

$$\frac{\text{minuts}}{\text{ounces}} \frac{8}{6} \times \frac{4}{x}$$

$$\frac{8x}{8} = \frac{24}{8}$$

$$3 \text{ ounces}$$

Fig. 1.1. Bonita's work on a proportion problem

Reflect 1.1

Do you think Bonita's work in figure 1.1 shows that she was reasoning proportionally? If so, why do you think so? If not, what do you think she may not have understood?

Bonita's work offers much to like. It is well organized. Bonita labeled the quantities of time and water in her proportion and correctly carried out the cross-multiplication procedure. However, Bonita's responses to three additional tasks suggest that she might not have understood important ideas related to proportional reasoning.

A second task called on Bonita to find the number of ounces that would drip through the same faucet in 40 minutes. To determine whether or not Bonita was procedurally bound to the cross-multiplication method, the interviewer asked her to solve the problem mentally or to use paper and pencil but without applying the algorithm. Bonita was at a loss. She said she couldn't do the problem in her head, and she was unable to do it on paper either. Even after the interviewer changed the specified time from 40 minutes to 16 minutes, Bonita was apparently unable to perform the simple act of doubling mentally or was unaware that doubling would be a reasonable approach.

A third task asked Bonita to solve a problem not posed in the typical form of three numbers given and one missing:

> Crystal placed a bucket under a faucet and collected 6 ounces of water in 20 minutes. Joanne placed a bucket under a second faucet and collected 3 ounces of water in 10 minutes. Were the faucets dripping equally fast or was one dripping faster than the other?

From what you have read so far about Bonita's reasoning, would you expect Bonita to come up with a way to solve this problem? Reflect 1.2 asks you to speculate about Bonita's thinking.

Reflect 1.2

How do you think Bonita approached the third task set for her by the interviewer? Do you think she was able to reason about it proportionally? Why or why not?

Bonita presented two solutions. First, she said that Crystal's faucet was dripping more slowly than Joanne's because "it took its time." This response suggests that Bonita compared only the amounts of time. Because 20 minutes is greater than 10 minutes, Bonita reasoned that the faucet taking more time was dripping more slowly than the faucet taking less time. Then Bonita changed her mind and said that Crystal's faucet was dripping faster because both amounts—time and water—for Crystal's faucet were greater than the corresponding amounts for Joanne's faucet (i.e., 20 > 10, and 6 > 3).

Bonita's response indicates that she did not form a ratio between the amount of water and the amount of time. In her first solution, she considered only one quantity—elapsed time. In her second attempt, she applied whole-number reasoning to two disconnected pairs of numbers. Bonita's response illustrates the difficulty that many middle school students experience in conceiving that something may remain the same while the values of the two quantities change.

The fourth and final task presented Bonita with the data shown in figure 1.2. She was told that another girl, Cassandra, had collected the data to see how fast her bathtub faucet was leaking. Cassandra had put a large container under the faucet in the morning and then had checked periodically throughout the day to see how much water was in the container. The interviewer constructed the table with uneven time intervals to approximate actual data collection but provided numbers that readily permitted mental calculations.

Time	Amount of Water
7:00 a.m.	2 ounces
8:15 a.m.	12 ounces
9:45 a.m.	24 ounces
2:30 p.m.	62 ounces
5:15 p.m.	84 ounces
6:00 p.m.	90 ounces
9:30 p.m.	118 ounces

Fig. 1.2. Data collected from a dripping bathtub faucet

To help Bonita comprehend the situation before encountering any difficult questions, the interviewer asked her how much water dripped between 7 a.m. and 8:15 a.m. Although this question required only simple subtraction (12 – 2 = 10), Bonita inappropriately set up a proportion and attempted to solve for x, as shown in figure 1.3. This work strongly suggests that Bonita did not understand when it is appropriate to compare numbers by forming a ratio. In sum, although Bonita could correctly execute the proportion algorithm on the first task, her work on the next three tasks demonstrates her poor conceptual understanding.

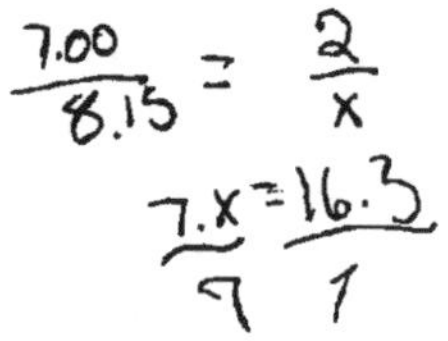

$$\frac{7.00}{8.15} = \frac{2}{x}$$

$$7 \cdot x = 16.3$$

$$\frac{7}{7} \quad \frac{1}{1}$$

Fig. 1.3. Bonita's work on the bathtub task

If Bonita had understood the ideas behind her work, then she should have been able to reason about the faucet that drips 6 ounces of water in 8 minutes by using at least one of the two following methods.

Proportional Reasoning Method 1

Bonita might have used the method described below to reason about the faucet that dripped 6 ounces in 8 minutes:

- Form a ratio by joining 6 ounces and 8 minutes into a single unit: *6 ounces in 8 minutes.*

- Iterate (repeat) this unit by reasoning that if the faucet drips another 6 ounces in 8 minutes, it does not speed up or slow down since the amounts of time and water are identical. Thus, a faucet that drips 12 ounces in 16 minutes drips at the same rate as one that drips 6 ounces in 8 minutes.

- Similarly, partition, or split, the "6 ounces in 8 minutes" unit in half. A faucet that drips 3 ounces in 4 minutes drips at the same rate as one that drips 6 ounces in 8 minutes.

- Make more challenging partitions. To determine the amount of water that drips in 1 minute, split the unit into eighths by finding $1/8$ of 6 ounces, which is $6/8$, or $3/4$, ounce, and by finding $1/8$ of 8 minutes, which is 1 minute. Thus, a faucet that drips $3/4$ ounce in 1 minute drips at the same rate as one that drips 6 ounces in 8 minutes.

- Combine the actions of iterating and partitioning. For example, quadruple the "6 ounces in 8 minutes" unit to obtain 24 ounces in 32 minutes. Also partition the "6 ounces in 8 minutes" unit into thirds by finding $1/3$ of 6 ounces, which is 2 ounces, and by finding $1/3$ of 8 minutes, which is $8/3$, or $2\,2/3$ minutes. Combine these results to obtain 26 ounces in $34\,2/3$ minutes, which is $4\,1/3$ times the "6 ounces in 8 minutes" unit.

In this manner, construct a large collection of ratios, all of which represent the same dripping rate: 6 ounces in 8 minutes,

12 ounces in 16 minutes, 3 ounces in 4 minutes, $3/4$ ounce in 1 minute, 26 ounces in $34 2/3$ minutes, and so on.

Proportional Reasoning Method 2

Alternatively, Bonita might have reasoned about the faucet dripping 6 ounces of water in 8 minutes by using the following method:

- Compare the two numerical values 6 and 8 (from 6 ounces in 8 minutes) by finding how many times greater 8 is than 6. Eight is $1 1/3$ times greater than 6.

- To determine the amount of time that it takes for any amount of water to drip, multiply the value of the water amount by $1 1/3$. For example, for 3 ounces of water, it will take $3 \times 1 1/3$, or 4, minutes. For 12 ounces, it will take $12 \times 1 1/3$, or 16, minutes.

- Construct a collection of ratios by maintaining the factor of $1 1/3$. That is, the water amount is always $1 1/3$ times greater than the time amount.

- Also compare the values 6 and 8 by finding what fraction 6 is of 8. Six is $6/8$, or $3/4$, of 8.

- To determine the amount of water that drips for any amount of time, multiply the time amount by $3/4$. For example, in 16 minutes, $16 \times 3/4$, or 12, ounces, of water will drip. In 4 minutes, $4 \times 3/4$, or 3, ounces of water will drip.

One Big Idea and Multiple Essential Understandings

The two methods that Bonita could have used to reason proportionally about the faucet dripping 6 ounces in 8 minutes suggest the following big idea related to ratios, proportions, and proportional reasoning: When two quantities are related proportionally, the ratio of one quantity to the other is invariant as the numerical values of both quantities change by the same factor.

In the situation of the dripping faucet, the water and time values change; yet, infinitely many water and time pairs represent the same dripping rate (e.g., 6 ounces in 8 minutes, 9 ounces in 12 minutes, 3 ounces in 4 minutes, $3/4$ ounce in 1 minute). Any pair in the collection of water and time pairs can be obtained by iterating and/or partitioning any other pair. For example, 9 ounces in 12 minutes is $1 1/2$ groups of 6 ounces in 8 minutes and is equal to 3 groups of 3 ounces in 4 minutes. Furthermore, the ratio of time to water in each pair is constant: the number of minutes is $1 1/3$ times the number of

When two quantities are related proportionally, the ratio of one quantity to the other is invariant as the numerical values of both quantities change by the same factor.

ounces. The ratio of water to time is also constant: the number of ounces is $3/4$ the number of minutes.

Although the big idea of proportionality may at first seem straightforward, developing an understanding of it is a complex process for students. It involves grasping many essential understandings:

Essential Understanding 1. Reasoning with ratios involves attending to and coordinating two quantities.

Essential Understanding 2. A ratio is a multiplicative comparison of two quantities, or it is a joining of two quantities in a composed unit.

Essential Understanding 3. Forming a ratio as a measure of a real-world attribute involves isolating that attribute from other attributes and understanding the effect of changing each quantity on the attribute of interest.

Essential Understanding 4. A number of mathematical connections link ratios and fractions:

- Ratios are often expressed in fraction notation, although ratios and fractions do not have identical meaning.
- Ratios are often used to make "part-part" comparisons, but fractions are not.
- Ratios and fractions can be thought of as overlapping sets.
- Ratios can often be meaningfully reinterpreted as fractions.

Essential Understanding 5. Ratios can be meaningfully reinterpreted as quotients.

Essential Understanding 6. A proportion is a relationship of equality between two ratios. In a proportion, the ratio of two quantities remains constant as the corresponding values of the quantities change.

Essential Understanding 7. Proportional reasoning is complex and involves understanding that—

- Equivalent ratios can be created by iterating and/or partitioning a composed unit;
- If one quantity in a ratio is multiplied or divided by a particular factor, then the other quantity must be multiplied or divided by the same factor to maintain the proportional relationship; and
- The two types of ratios—composed units and multiplicative comparisons—are related.

Essential Understanding 8. A rate is a set of infinitely many equivalent ratios.

Essential Understanding 9. Several ways of reasoning, all grounded in sense making, can be generalized into algorithms for solving proportion problems.

Essential Understanding 10. Superficial cues present in the context of a problem do not provide sufficient evidence of proportional relationships between quantities.

The purpose of this chapter is to elaborate and develop these essential understandings, which were implicit in the discussion of Bonita's work. The discussion moves from ratios to proportions (pairs of equivalent ratios) and finally to proportional reasoning (which involves generating an entire set of equivalent ratios). The chart in figure 1.4 illustrates the flow of ideas. Notice that each essential understanding provides a response to a different question. However, the chart is not meant to show the order in which all students develop these ideas.

The initial cluster of essential understandings deals with ratios, because ratios are a building block for the formation of proportions and proportional reasoning. The first essential understanding addresses how ratio reasoning differs from non-ratio reasoning.

Essential Understanding	Question	Topic
1	How does ratio reasoning differ from other types of reasoning?	Ratios
2	What is a ratio?	
3	What is a ratio as a measure of an attribute in a real-world situation?	
4	How are ratios related to fractions?	
5	How are ratios related to division?	
6	What is a proportion?	Proportions
7	What are the key aspects of proportional reasoning?	Proportional Reasoning
8	What is a rate and how is it related to proportional reasoning?	
9	What is the relationship between the cross-multiplication algorithm and proportional reasoning?	
10	When is it appropriate to reason proportionally?	

Fig. 1.4. Organization of the essential understandings developed in chapter 1

Essential Understanding 1

Reasoning with ratios involves attending to and coordinating two quantities.

Attending to two quantities is an aspect of reasoning with ratios that mathematically knowledgeable adults understand so implicitly that they often do not recognize its importance until they become aware of its absence in the reasoning of children. Before children are able to reason with ratios, they typically reason with a single quantity. This type of reasoning is called *univariate reasoning*. Harel and colleagues (1994) offer an example of this reasoning. Sixth-grade students were shown a picture of a carton of orange juice and were told that the juice was made from orange concentrate and water. Next to the carton in the picture were two glasses—a large glass and a small glass—both filled with orange juice from the carton. The sixth graders were asked if they thought that the orange juice from the two glasses would taste equally orangey, or if they thought that the juice in one glass would taste more orangey than the juice in the other.

The results are fascinating. Half the class responded incorrectly that the juice from the two glasses would not be equally orangey. About half of these students said that the juice in the large glass would taste more orangey, and about half chose the small glass as likely to taste more orangey. Their explanations suggest that they either focused on one quantity—the water or the orange concentrate—or attended to both quantities but did not coordinate them. For example, one student explained that the juice in the large glass would taste more orangey "because the glass is bigger, so it would hold more orange" (p. 333). Other students explained that the juice in the small glass would taste more orangey because a smaller volume would allow less water to get in, which would leave more room for the orange concentrate.

The importance of coordinating two quantities becomes clear in the following example, which shows the intellectual achievement that such coordination can represent for children. In a study by Lobato and Thanheiser (2002), students in a class viewed a computer screen with SimCalc Mathworlds software showing two characters—a clown and a frog—capable of being set to walk at constant speeds. The clown was set to walk 10 centimeters in 4 seconds. The children were asked to enter distance and time values for the frog so that it would walk at the same speed as the clown (see fig. 1.5). The simulation software would then show the two journeys simultaneously, thus providing feedback that students could use to determine whether the values that they entered were correct. This activity presented a challenge for the students. Many used a guess-and-check strategy; for example, one student tried 15 centimeters and 8 seconds and then kept adjusting the time until he arrived at 15 centimeters in 6 seconds. Other students used numeric patterns—for example, doubling the 10 and the 4 to obtain 20 centimeters in 8 seconds.

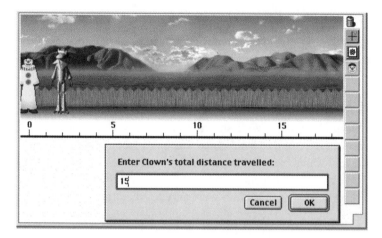

Fig. 1.5. A screen from Roschelle and Kaput's (1996) SimCalc Mathworlds

When the teacher asked the students to explain why walking 20 centimeters in 8 seconds is the same speed as walking 10 centimeters in 4 seconds, one student, Terry, created a drawing that suggests that he had not formed a ratio. Figure 1.6 shows a re-creation of his diagram. He drew lines to represent the distances walked by the two characters without attempting to show that the frog's distance was double the clown's distance. He then relied on calculations, stating, "If you want frog's distance to be 20, then you have to multiply 10 by 2 to get 20. Since you multiplied 10 by 2, you also need to multiply 4 by 2 to get 8." Terry did not explain *why* the time and distance had to be doubled or how multiplying by two could be represented in his drawing.

clown	10
frog	

Fig. 1.6. A re-creation of Terry's diagram

Jim, the next student to go to the board, offered a limited explanation that was nearly identical to Terry's. The discussion appeared to stall, when suddenly another student—Brad—had a new idea that he seemed eager to share. Brad explained that doubling works as follows:

Because the clown is walking the same distance; it's just that he's walking the distance twice... he's walking it once, going li, li, li, li, li, li, [Brad made a "li" sound, evidently to represent time, while his hand retraced the 10 cm line that Terry had drawn], all the way to here [Brad made a vertical hash mark at 10 cm]. Four seconds. Okay. He's going to walk it again. Another four seconds, li, li, li, li, li, li, li. Another ten centimeters in four seconds. He's done. (Lobato and Thanheiser 2002, p. 173)

Brad's explanation involved three elements lacking in both Terry's and Jim's work. First, Brad appeared to coordinate time and distance by using sound to represent time while using a hand gesture to represent distance. Second, Brad seemed to coordinate distance and time by forming a "10 centimeters in 4 seconds chunk," which he could repeat. In contrast, Terry seemed to pick one quantity—namely, 20 centimeters—and then produced the other related quantity of 8 seconds. Finally, Brad's image accounted for the frog after the initial 10 centimeters in 4 seconds by noting that the frog walks another 10 centimeters in 4 seconds. By repeating the action of walking 10 centimeters in 4 seconds, the frog will not go faster or slower but will walk at the same speed in both journeys, as well as in the combined journey. In contrast, Terry's explanation did not account for how far the frog walked and in what time after the clown had stopped.

As necessary as it is for students to coordinate two quantities in their reasoning, doing so is not sufficient for understanding ratios. For example, it is possible for students to coordinate two quantities by engaging in a form of reasoning that is different from ratio reasoning—namely, *additive reasoning.* Consider the following situation:

Jonathan has walked 5 feet in 4 seconds. How long should Rafael take to walk 15 feet if he walks at the same speed as Jonathan?

A seventh grader, Miriam, responded that Rafael should take 14 seconds. She reasoned that 15 feet is 10 more than 5 feet, so you should add 10 seconds to 4 seconds to get 14 seconds. Miriam accounted for both time and distance, but her reasoning was additive because it focused on questions related to "how much more" or "how much less" one quantity is than another. Miriam's work raises the question of what it means to form a ratio.

Essential Understanding 2

A ratio is a multiplicative comparison of two quantities, or it is a joining of two quantities in a composed unit.

There are two ways to form a ratio, both of which involve coordinating two quantities. One way is by comparing two quantities multiplicatively. The second way is by joining or composing the two quantities in a way that preserves a multiplicative relationship.

A ratio as a multiplicative comparison

One way to form a ratio is to create a *multiplicative comparison of two quantities*. For example, consider comparing the lengths of the two worms in figure 1.7. Worm A is 6 inches long, and worm B is 4 inches long. The lengths of the worms can be compared in two ways—additively and multiplicatively. *Additive comparisons* of the lengths would pose and answer questions such as the following:

- How much longer is worm A than worm B?
  (Worm A is 2 inches longer than worm B.)

- How much shorter is worm B than worm A?
  (Worm B is 2 inches shorter than worm A.)

By contrast, *multiplicative comparisons* would consider questions like those below:

- How many times longer is worm A than worm B? (Worm A is $1\frac{1}{2}$ times the length of worm B.)

- The length of worm B is what part, or fraction, of the length of worm A? (Worm B is $\frac{2}{3}$ the length of worm A.)

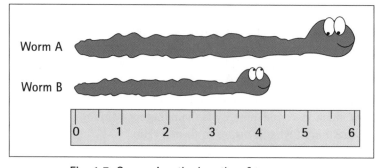

Fig. 1.7. Comparing the lengths of two worms

A multiplicative comparison is a ratio; an additive comparison is not. In general, forming a multiplicative comparison involves asking, "How many times greater is one thing than another?" or "What part or fraction is one thing of another?"

Mathematics uses several conventional notations to represent ratios. You might write the ratio of the length of worm A to the length of worm B as $1^1/_2 : 1$, $1^1/_2$ to 1, or simply $1^1/_2$. You could also report equivalent ratios, such as $3 : 2$, 3 to 2, or $3/_2$, as well as $6 : 4$, 6 to 4, or $6/_4$. You could express the ratio of the lengths of worm B to worm A as $2 : 3$, 2 to 3, or $2/_3$, as well as $4 : 6$, 4 to 6, or $4/_6$, in addition to $1 : 1^1/_2$ or 1 to $1^1/_2$.

A ratio as a composed unit

Another way to form a ratio is by *composing* (joining) two quantities to create a new unit. Evidence of the formation of a *composed unit* often appears in a student's iterating (repeating) or partitioning (breaking apart into equal-sized sections) of a composed unit. Brad's iterating of "10 centimeters in 4 seconds" in the earlier example involving the clown and the frog offers evidence of his formation of a composed unit.

In fact, Brad's discovery led to a flurry of activity, in which other students used the 10 : 4 unit to create new "same speed" values. For example, Denise iterated the 10 : 4 unit three times to conclude that walking 30 centimeters in 12 seconds was the same speed as walking 10 centimeters in 4 seconds. Terry partitioned the 10 : 4 unit into four equal parts, formed a new composed unit of 2.5 : 1 (indicated by the shaded section in fig. 1.8), and then iterated the 2.5 : 1 unit four times to re-create 10 centimeters in 4 seconds. He explained why walking 2.5 centimeters in 1 second was the same speed as walking 10 centimeters in 4 seconds by stating, "It would be like he's walking one-fourth of the 10 and 4; it's like one-fourth of each thing," meaning $1/_4$ of the 10 centimeters and $1/_4$ of the 4 seconds.

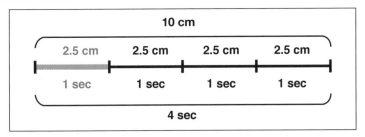

Fig. 1.8. A diagram showing that walking 2.5 centimeters in 1 second is the same speed as walking 10 centimeters in 4 seconds (Lobato and Thanheiser 2002, p. 174)

Forming a ratio as a composed unit does not by itself mean that the student has attained the sophisticated understanding of proportionality that is reflected in the big idea of ratios, proportions, and proportional reasoning. Forming a composed unit is a rudimentary, yet foundational concept, which can be used in conjunction with other essential understandings (especially Essential Understanding 7) to develop an understanding of the big idea of proportional reasoning.

How do the two ways of thinking about a ratio—as a multiplicative comparison and as a composed unit—help in problem solving? Reflect 1.3 encourages you to consider the usefulness of the two concepts of a ratio expressed in Essential Understanding 2.

Reflect 1.3

Suppose that you have made a batch of green paint by mixing 2 cans of blue paint with 7 cans of yellow paint. What are some other combinations of numbers of cans of blue paint and yellow paint that you can mix to make the same shade of green? Solve the problem in two different ways—first by using a multiplicative comparison and then by using a composed unit.

→ Essential Understanding 7

Proportional reasoning is complex and involves understanding that—

- *equivalent ratios can be created by iterating and/ or partitioning a composed unit;*

- *if one quantity in a ratio is multiplied or divided by a particular factor, then the other quantity must be multiplied or divided by the same factor to maintain the proportional relationship; and*

- *the two types of ratios—composed units and multiplicative comparisons—are related.*

You can use a picture like that in figure 1.9 to solve the problem by using a multiplicative comparison. First, determine how many times greater the amount of yellow paint is than the amount of blue paint in the original batch of green paint. One way to do this is to form a group of 2 cans of blue paint. Then find the number of groups of 2 cans that you can make with 7 cans. It takes $3^1/_2$ groups of 2 cans of blue paint to match the amount of yellow paint (see fig. 1.10). Thus, the ratio of yellow paint to blue paint is $3^1/_2$ or 3.5.

Fig. 1.9. Two cans of blue paint and 7 cans of yellow paint

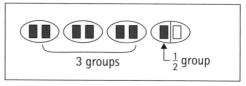

Fig. 1.10. Three-and-a-half groups of 2 cans of blue paint yield an amount equal to the amount of yellow paint in the original batch.

You can use this ratio to find other combinations of blue and yellow paint that result in the same shade of green paint. For example, if you use 5 cans of blue paint, then you need to mix in $3^1/_2$ times as many cans of yellow paint. As shown in figure 1.11, $3^1/_2$ groups of 5 cans are equal to $17^1/_2$ cans. Thus, one way to make a new batch of paint in the same shade of green as the original batch is to use 5 cans of blue paint and $17^1/_2$ cans of yellow paint.

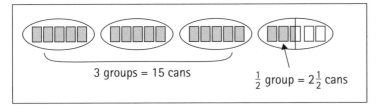

Fig. 1.11. The number of cans of paint in $3\frac{1}{2}$ groups of 5 cans

You can also solve the paint problem by using a composed unit. First, join 2 cans of blue paint and 7 cans of yellow paint to form a 2:7 unit, or batch (see fig. 1.12). Then iterate or partition the 2:7 batch to find the number of cans of yellow paint that you need for 5 cans of blue paint. Iterating the 2:7 batch twice gives you 4 cans of blue paint and 14 cans of yellow paint. Because you need one more can of blue paint, partition the 2:7 batch into two equal parts to obtain 1 can of blue paint

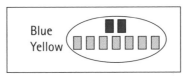

Fig. 1.12. A composed unit of 2 cans of blue paint and 7 cans of yellow paint

and $3\frac{1}{2}$ cans of yellow paint, as in figure 1.13. In all, $2\frac{1}{2}$ batches of paint require 5 cans of blue paint and $17\frac{1}{2}$ cans of yellow paint.

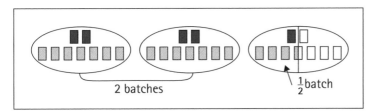

Fig. 1.13. Two-and-a-half batches of green paint,
made with 5 cans of blue paint

The notion of a ratio in Essential Understanding 2 as a multiplicative comparison or a composed unit may differ from definitions of ratio in some textbooks. For example, a ratio is commonly defined as a comparison of two quantities. Such a definition is incomplete because it does not clarify whether the comparison is additive or multiplicative.

A ratio is also sometimes defined as a comparison of two numbers that uses division and is often expressed in fraction form. This definition leads students to write expressions such as a/b or $a \div b$. However, this definition has several shortcomings. First, it is possible to form a ratio without performing division or creating a fraction. Second, simply by writing "a/b" or "$a \div b$," a student gives no guarantee that he or she has actually mentally formed a ratio between *a* and *b*.

For instance, consider the middle school task shown in figure 1.14 in the context of making orange juice by mixing cans of orange concentrate with cans of water. Each purple rectangle in the figure represents a can of concentrate, and each white rectangle represents an equal quantity of water. The student must determine the ratio of concentrate to water in the orange juice.

Fig. 1.14. A typical middle school ratio task

Suppose that a student correctly writes "$^2/_3$" or enters "2 ÷ 3" into a calculator to obtain approximately 0.667. This performance does not mean that he or she understands the situation as involving a ratio; it may simply represent a whole-number counting strategy. The student may count the number of cans of orange concentrate, count the number of cans of water, and write a 2 "over" a 3, without understanding the meaning of $^2/_3$. In fact, many seventh graders can correctly write $^2/_3$ in this situation but do not demonstrate an ability to reason with ratios in response to a simple follow-up question:

> Does a batch of orange juice made with 2 cans of orange concentrate and 3 cans of water taste equally orangey, more orangey, or less orangey than a batch made with 4 cans of orange concentrate and 6 cans of water?

Typical responses that indicate an inadequate understanding of ratios include (*a*) "the second batch is more orangey because both numbers are bigger" and (*b*) "the second batch tastes more orangey because you used more orange concentrate." By writing "$^2/_3$," students can give the illusion that they have a greater understanding of ratio than is actually the case. Remember, *forming a ratio is a cognitive task—not a writing task*. And finally, note that defining a ratio in terms of division places an emphasis on numeric calculations. Essential Understanding 3 highlights an important mathematical idea that does not involve numbers but is related to the formation of ratios in real-world situations.

Essential Understanding 3

Forming a ratio as a measure of a real-world attribute involves isolating that attribute from other attributes and understanding the effect of changing each quantity on the attribute of interest.

In many of the examples of ratio presented thus far, the ratio measures some attribute in a real-world situation. For example, the ratio of orange concentrate to water is a measure of the *oranginess* of the juice. The ratio of the height of a wheelchair ramp to the length of its base is a measure of the *steepness* of the ramp. Simon and Blume (1994) coined the term "ratio-as-measure" for a ratio that measures some real-world attribute. Forming a "ratio-as-measure" involves two non-numerical processes: (*a*) isolating attributes and (*b*) understanding the effect of changing a quantity on the attribute to be measured by the ratio. The following discussion considers each of these in turn.

Isolating attributes

Before someone can use a ratio to measure an attribute, he or she needs to isolate the attribute from other measurable attributes in the situation. Seeing how difficult it can be for students to isolate attributes can help convey the significance of this essential understanding.

   In one study, seventeen high school students were asked to create a way to measure the steepness of a wheelchair ramp (Lobato 2008). Although the students had recently received instruction in slope, they did not automatically measure the height and base of the ramp and form a ratio. More than half of the students struggled to isolate the attribute of steepness from other attributes, such as the work required to climb the ramp. Many students talked about the importance of including the length of the slanted part of the ramp in their measure of steepness, arguing that a longer ramp is more difficult to climb; a person slows down as he or she moves up the ramp.

   To gain a better understanding of this difficulty, consider the two nonidentical ramps with the same steepness in figure 1.15.

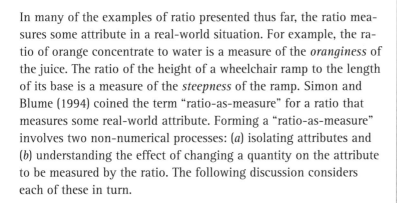

Fig. 1.15. Two nonidentical ramps with the same steepness

Students might argue that the ramp on the right is steeper because it is higher, longer, or harder to climb. For example, if students do not isolate the attribute of steepness from the attribute of the work required to climb the ramp, then they might conclude incorrectly that the ramps do not have the same steepness, because people will become more tired when climbing the ramp on the right.

Understanding the effect of changing a quantity

Students need to understand which quantities affect the attribute to be measured by a ratio and how the quantities affect it. Again consider the situation of a wheelchair ramp. If students form a ratio of the height to the base of the ramp, then the attribute that the ratio measures is the steepness of the ramp. In the case of a ramp with a platform at the top, the students need to understand that decreasing the length of the base of the ramp (while leaving its height and platform unchanged) will increase the steepness of the ramp, but increasing the length of the base will decrease its steepness, as illustrated in the first and second changes to the original ramp in figure 1.16. Similarly, increasing the height of the ramp (while leaving the base unchanged) will increase the steepness of the ramp, but decreasing the height will decrease its steepness, as illustrated in the third and fourth changes in the figure. Increasing or decreasing the length of the platform will not change the steepness of the ramp (the last change in the figure shows an increase in the length of the platform).

One of the authors found that a majority of high school students in a study (Lobato 2008) had difficulty determining the effect of changing one quantity at a time on the steepness of the ramp. Students were able to reason correctly that increasing the height made the ramp steeper and decreasing the height made the ramp less steep. However, over half of the students were unable to determine the effect of increasing or decreasing the length of the base or the platform. For example, one student argued that making the length of the base shorter makes the ramp less steep, and making the base longer makes the ramp steeper. These difficulties point to the importance of Essential Understanding 3.

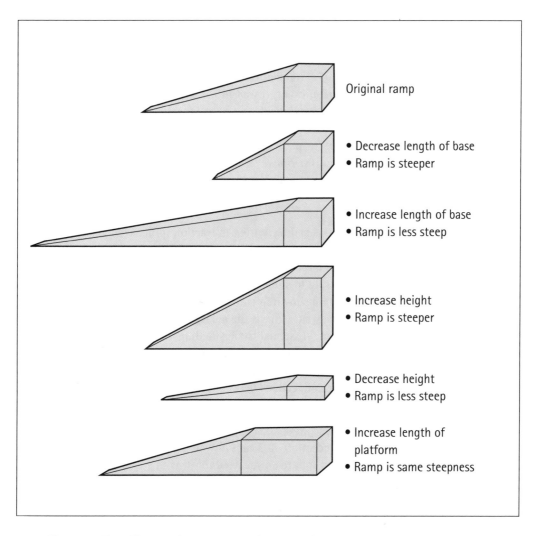

Original ramp

- Decrease length of base
- Ramp is steeper

- Increase length of base
- Ramp is less steep

- Increase height
- Ramp is steeper

- Decrease height
- Ramp is less steep

- Increase length of platform
- Ramp is same steepness

Fig. 1.16. The effect on the steepness of a ramp of changing one quantity at a time

Essential Understanding 4

A number of mathematical connections link ratios and fractions:
- *Ratios are often expressed in fraction notation, although ratios and fractions do not have identical meaning.*
- *Ratios are often used to make "part-part" comparisons, but fractions are not.*
- *Ratios and fractions can be thought of as overlapping sets.*
- *Ratios can often be meaningfully reinterpreted as fractions.*

Interpreting a fraction as a ratio is one of several interpretations of fractions discussed in Developing Essential Understanding of Rational Numbers for Teaching Mathematics in Grades 3–5 *(Barnett-Clarke et al., forthcoming).*

Because ratios can be written in fraction form as $^a/_b$, many students believe that *ratio* is just another word for *fraction*. The use of fraction language in discussions of problems involving ratios can be particularly confusing to students. For example, in discussing the solution to the proportion shown in connection with the problem in figure 1.17, a teacher may say, "Six is the answer because $^2/_3$ and $^6/_9$ are equivalent fractions." Essential Understanding 4 highlights the mathematical connections between ratios and fractions. The notation $^a/_b$ can easily cloud students' understanding of ratios if the students have not yet grasped the connections between ratios and fractions.

> If you make orange juice in the ratio of 2 cans of orange concentrate to 3 cans of water, how many cans of orange concentrate do you need to use with 9 cans of water?
>
> $$\frac{2}{3} = \frac{x}{9}$$

Fig. 1.17. A typical textbook problem expressed as a proportion

Ratios and fractions do not have identical meanings. Ratios are often used to make part-part comparisons, though fractions are not. For example, consider a salad dressing that is 2 parts vinegar to 5 parts oil. The *ratio* of vinegar to oil is expressed as 2 : 5, 2 to 5, or $^2/_5$. In this context, $^2/_5$ is a part-part comparison. In contrast, the *fraction* of the salad dressing that is oil is $^5/_7$, which is a part-whole comparison, and the fraction that is vinegar is $^2/_7$, which is another part-whole comparison.

Ratios and fractions can be conceived as overlapping sets (Clark, Berenson, and Cavey 2003). An example of a ratio that is not a fraction is the *golden ratio*

$$(\frac{\sqrt{5}+1}{2}).$$

This ratio is an irrational number, whereas fractions are rational numbers. A second example of a ratio that is not a fraction is the part-part comparison of vinegar to oil presented above—namely, $^2/_5$. Furthermore, ratios can involve more than two terms, such as the ratio of numbers of containers of whole milk to numbers of containers of low-fat milk to numbers of containers of nonfat milk in a certain store (e.g., $5:3:1$). In the intersection of the sets of ratios and fractions are ratios that are formed as part-whole comparisons, as illustrated in figure 1.18. For example, the ratio of vinegar to total ingredients in the salad dressing—namely, $2:7$—can also be thought of as a fraction: two-sevenths of the dressing is vinegar.

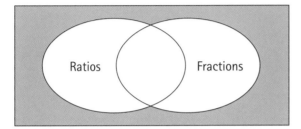

Fig. 1.18. Ratios and fractions as overlapping sets

At the other extreme are the various ways of thinking of fractions as entities other than part-whole comparisons. These ways include thinking of a fraction as a point on a number line (e.g., $^8/_9$ as a number between 0 and 1 on a number line). A fraction conceived in this way is often called a "fraction-as-measure." A fraction can also be thought of as an operator, such as a "shrinker" or "stretcher," which transforms the size of a given amount. Consider, for example, shrinking an amount by the fraction $^1/_3$. In neither case—fraction as measure or fraction as operator—is the fraction typically conceived as a ratio.

Despite the fact that ratios and fractions do not share identical meanings, many ratios can be meaningfully reinterpreted as fractions. Reconsider the 2 to 5 ratio of vinegar to oil in the salad dressing example. You can reinterpret this part-part comparison as a part-whole comparison (i.e., as two-fifths of something). Remember that the ratio $2:5$ does not indicate the exact amounts of vinegar or oil used in a particular recipe. The dressing could use 2 cups of vinegar and 5 cups of oil, 4 cups of vinegar and 10 cups of oil, 1 cup of vinegar and $2\,^1/_2$ cups of oil, and so forth. The recipe might also use 6 tablespoons of vinegar and 15 tablespoons of oil, $^1/_2$ pint of vinegar and $1\,^1/_4$ pints of oil, and so on. In each of these recipes, $^2/_5$ also has meaning as a fraction because each recipe calls for two-fifths as much vinegar as oil.

For example, consider a salad dressing recipe that calls for 4 cups of vinegar and 10 cups of oil. The fact that 4 is $^2/_5$ of 10 can be illustrated visually. Figure 1.19 separates the 10 cups into 5 equal groups, or fifths. One-fifth of 10 cups is 2 cups. Figure 1.20 then shows two one-fifths of 10 cups, or 4 cups. The amount of vinegar in this recipe (4 cups) is $^2/_5$ of the amount of oil (10 cups). In sum, the ratio $2:5$ can be reinterpreted as the fraction $^2/_5$, to mean that salad dressing made from this recipe always has $^2/_5$ as much vinegar as oil, no matter what particular amounts of vinegar and oil someone uses.

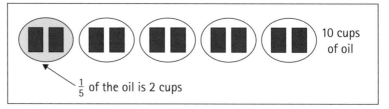

Fig. 1.19. One-fifth of 10 cups

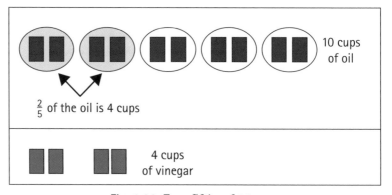

Fig. 1.20. Two-fifths of 10 cups

A second way to interpret the ratio $2:5$ as the fraction $^2/_5$ is possible. Suppose that you use 2 cups of vinegar and 5 cups of oil to make the salad dressing. Figure 1.21 shows the "joining" of the vinegar and oil to form a batch of salad dressing. You maintain the ratio $2:5$ if you partition the batch into 5 equal parts. Your partitioning of the batch partitions both the oil and vinegar into 5 equal parts. Splitting 5 cups of oil into 5 equal parts yields 1 cup of oil in each part. Splitting 2 cups of vinegar into 5 equal parts is more difficult. One way is to split the first cup of vinegar into 5 equal parts, which yields $^1/_5$ cup of oil in each part. By repeating this process with the second cup, you obtain another $^1/_5$ cup in each part. Altogether, if you partition 2 cups of oil into 5 equal parts, you have $^2/_5$ of a cup of oil in each part. Consequently, salad dressing made with $^2/_5$ cup of vinegar and 1 cup of oil, as illustrated in figure 1.22, maintains the $2:5$ ratio of vinegar to oil.

In sum, the ratio $2:5$ (meaning "2 parts vinegar to 5 parts oil") can be reinterpreted as the fraction $^2/_5$ in two different ways. The first way is to say that in this salad dressing recipe the amount of vinegar is always $^2/_5$ the amount of oil, no matter what particular amounts of vinegar and oil someone uses to make the dressing.

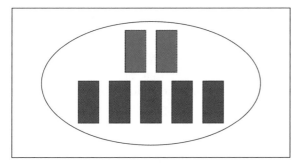

Fig. 1.21. A composed unit of 2 cups of vinegar and 5 cups of oil

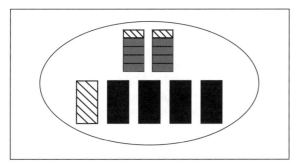

Fig. 1.22. One–fifth of the batch is $^2/_5$ cup of vinegar and 1 cup of oil

This interpretation is based on understanding the ratio 2 : 5 as a multiplicative comparison—namely, that 2 is $^2/_5$ of 5. The second way to interpret the ratio as a fraction is to think of the two-fifths as referring to the pairing of $^2/_5$ cup of vinegar with 1 cup of oil, which maintains the recipe. This interpretation is based on under-standing the ratio 2 : 5 as a composed unit, and then partitioning that unit into five equal parts. Reflect 1.4 invites you to apply these two ways of reinterpreting a ratio as a fraction in a different real-world context.

Reflect 1.4

Water is being pumped through a hose into a large swimming pool so that 3 gallons collect in the pool every 4 minutes. What are two different ways to reinterpret the ratio 3 : 4 as the fraction $^3/_4$ in this context? What are two ways to reinterpret the ratio 4 : 3 as the improper fraction $^4/_3$?

One way to reinterpret the ratio 3 : 4 (3 gallons every 4 min-utes) as the fraction $^3/_4$ is to say that the number of gallons of water in the pool is always $^3/_4$ of the number of minutes that have passed, assuming that the water continues to flow into the pool at a constant rate. For example, after 4 minutes, 3 gallons of water are in the pool, and 3 is $3/4$ of 4. Similarly, after 20 minutes, 15 gallons of water are in the pool, and 15 is $3/4$ of 20. This interpretation is based on thinking of the ratio $3:4$ as a multiplicative comparison—namely, that 3 is $3/4$ of 4. A second way to reinterpret the ratio $3:4$ as the fraction $3/4$ is to consider that $3/4$ of a gallon is the amount of water that needs to flow into the pool in 1 minute to maintain the same pumping rate. This interpretation is based on thinking of the ratio $3:4$ as a composed unit and then partitioning that unit into four equal parts.

The pumping rate can also be captured by the ratio $4:3$, meaning that 4 minutes elapse for every 3 gallons of water that are pumped into the pool. This ratio can be reinterpreted as the improper fraction $4/3$ in two ways. The first way is to say that the number of minutes that elapse is always $4/3$ times the number of gallons of water that has flowed into the pool in that time. For example, 12 gallons are pumped in 16 minutes, and $12 \times 4/3 = 16$. This interpretation is based on understanding the ratio $4:3$ as a multiplicative comparison—namely, that 4 is $4/3$ (or $1\,1/3$) times 3. The second way to reinterpret the ratio $4:3$ as the improper fraction $4/3$ is to consider that $4/3$ minutes is the amount of time that it takes to pump 1 gallon of water into the pool. This interpretation is based on joining 4 minutes and 3 gallons into a composed unit and partitioning that unit into three equal parts.

Essential Understanding 5

Ratios can be meaningfully reinterpreted as quotients.

Just as many ratios can be meaningfully reinterpreted as fractions, ratios can also be reinterpreted as quotients. For example, consider a situation in which a leaky faucet has been dripping all day. Suppose that 4 ounces of water drip every 2 minutes, a rate that is expressed by the ratio 4 : 2. If someone places a bucket under the faucet, he or she will collect 8 ounces of water after 4 minutes, 20 ounces after 10 minutes, 120 ounces after 1 hour, and so on. You can reinterpret the ratio 4 : 2 as the quotient 4 ÷ 2. One meaning of division is sharing. In the context of the leaky faucet, you can think of the number of ounces of water that have dripped as divvied up, or shared, among the number of minutes. Figure 1.23 illustrates 4 ÷ 2 as the equal sharing of 4 ounces of water between 2 minutes (much as 4 cookies might be shared between 2 people). Shaded arrows in the figure indicate the divvying-up process. The resulting quotient of 2 means that 2 ounces of water drip every minute.

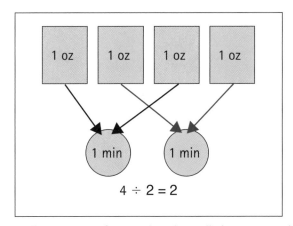

Fig. 1.23. Four ounces of water shared equally between 2 minutes

Consider the same situation again with a more difficult ratio. Suppose that 2 ounces of water drip every 5 minutes. Again, you can reinterpret the ratio—in this case, 2 : 5—as a quotient (2 ÷ 5) by thinking of the number of ounces of water (2) as shared among the number of minutes (5). Figure 1.24 illustrates the process. The first ounce is split into 5 equal parts so that $^1/_5$ ounce is associated with each of the 5 minutes. The second ounce is also split five ways, with another $^1/_5$ ounce being associated with each minute. In all, 2 one-fifths of an ounce, or $^2/_5$ of an ounce, is matched with each minute. Thus, in this situation the quotient 2 ÷ 5 means that $^2/_5$ of an ounce of water drips every minute, or, expressed as a decimal, 0.4 ounces of water drip per minute. Reinterpreting ratios as quotients can be useful in making sense of a proportion, which is an expression of equality between two ratios.

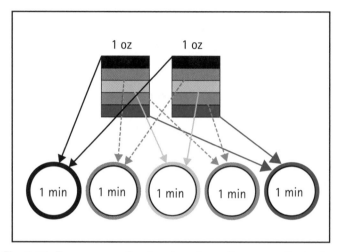

Fig. 1.24. Two ounces of water shared equally among 5 minutes

Essential Understanding 6

A proportion is a relationship of equality between two ratios. In a proportion, the ratio of two quantities remains constant as the corresponding values of the quantities change.

When textbooks call on students to solve a problem involving a proportion, they typically prompt the students to set up a proportion in the form shown in figure 1.25. However, students who have not yet mentally formed ratios, either as composed units or multiplicative comparisons, may interpret the proportion simply as a template for inserting whole numbers into boxes.

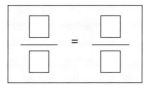

Fig. 1.25. A template for setting up a proportion

Consider again the situation involving equal walking speeds for the clown and the frog, discussed in connection with Essential Understanding 1:

The clown walks 10 centimeters in 4 seconds. How far will the frog walk in 8 seconds if the frog travels at the same speed as the clown?

Students might be able to set up a proportion correctly to solve the problem:

$$\frac{\text{Distance (cm)}}{\text{Time (sec)}} \qquad \frac{10}{4} = \frac{x}{8}$$

They might be able to use the proportion to determine correctly that the frog walked 20 centimeters. Yet, they might not have mentally formed a ratio. Many middle school students might harbor the thought that the frog is actually going faster than the clown because he is going farther—an example of univariate reasoning, as discussed earlier—or because both numbers on the frog's "side" of the proportion—20 and 8—are bigger than the corresponding numbers on the clown's side—an example of whole-number reasoning. It is difficult for many middle school students to conceive that something in the situation remains the same while the distance and time values are changing.

Understanding that a proportion is a relationship of equality between two ratios involves several related ideas. First, students

Essential Understanding 1

Reasoning with ratios involves attending to and coordinating two quantities.

need to understand the meaning of the equals sign in the symbolic expression of the proportion. Reflect 1.5 encourages you to focus on the meaning of equality in this context.

Reflect 1.5

Consider the proportion involved in the problem of the clown that walks 10 centimeters in 4 seconds and the frog that walks 20 centimeters in 8 seconds: $^{10}/_4 = {}^{20}/_8$. What is the meaning of the equals sign in this context? In other words, what is equal in the walking situation?

➡️ **Essential Understanding 5**

Ratios can be meaningfully reinterpreted as quotients.

In this context, the equals sign indicates that the *speeds* of the clown and the frog are the same. By applying Essential Understanding 5, you can reinterpret the ratios $^{10}/_4$ and $^{20}/_8$ as the quotients $10 \div 4$ and $20 \div 8$, respectively, both of which represent a speed of 2.5 centimeters per second.

Making sense of the proportion $^{10}/_4 = {}^{20}/_8$ requires an understanding of additional ideas. Teachers sometimes give meaning to the equality by pointing out to their students that the fraction $^{20}/_8$ can be reduced to the fraction $^{10}/_4$. However, it is important to realize that students can reduce fractions by employing an algorithm that requires only whole-number understanding—that is, they can divide 20 by 2 and 8 by 2. Students who work in this way have not necessarily conceived of 10:4 and 20:8 as ratios representing the same speed. Furthermore, simply calling a ratio a fraction gives no guarantee that students can meaningfully reinterpret ratios as fractions. Instead, they need to have a reliable understanding of one of the meanings of a fraction articulated in Essential Understanding 4.

➡️ *Ratios can often be meaningfully reinterpreted as fractions (from Essential Understanding 4).*

For example, the ratio 10 : 4 can be reinterpreted as a fraction in the walking context—namely, as $^{10}/_4$ centimeters in 1 second (i.e., ten one-fourths of a centimeter in 1 second). This fractional interpretation of the ratio 10:4 is based on joining 10 centimeters and 4 seconds into a composed unit and partitioning the unit into four equal parts. Partitioning 4 seconds into four equal parts yields 1 second in each part. Partitioning 10 centimeters into four equal parts involves splitting each centimeter into fourths and gathering $^1/_4$ from each centimeter for a total of 10 one-fourths, or $^{10}/_4$, centimeters in each part. Thus, the fraction $^{10}/_4$ represents the distance that the clown or the frog walks in 1 second. Similarly, the ratio 20 : 8 can be reinterpreted as $^{20}/_8$ centimeters in 1 second. Seeing that the fractions $^{10}/_4$ and $^{20}/_8$ represent the same distance walked in 1 second involves reasoning such as the following: Because $^1/_8$ is half of $^1/_4$, two one-eighths is equal to $^1/_4$. Thus ten groups of $^2/_8$ will equal the value of ten groups of $^1/_4$, so $^{20}/_8 = {}^{10}/_4$.

Reflect 1.6 gives you an opportunity to consider a new proportion in the salad dressing context discussed earlier and to explain its meaning by reinterpreting its ratios as fractions and by considering the meaning of the equals sign in this context.

Reflect 1.6

Consider the following proportion arising in the context of making a salad dressing:

$$\frac{\text{Vinegar}}{\text{Oil}} \quad \frac{2}{3} = \frac{10}{15}$$

What is the meaning of this statement in the context?

The equals sign indicates that two batches of salad dressing (one made from 2 parts vinegar and 3 parts oil and the other made from 10 parts vinegar and 15 parts oil) are equally vinegary, meaning that they will taste the same. To understand why this is the case, you can reinterpret the ratios $2:3$ and $10:15$ as fractions. Specifically, the fraction $2/3$ means that a recipe made from $2/3$ of a cup of vinegar and 1 cup of oil will maintain the $2:3$ ratio, thus preserving the taste. Similarly, a salad dressing made from $10/15$ of a cup of vinegar and 1 cup of oil will preserve the $10:15$ ratio. To establish that $2/3$ of a cup is equal to $10/15$ of a cup, think of $15/15$ as $5/15 + 5/15 + 5/15$. Each group of 5 one-fifteenths is equal to $1/3$ cup because $15/15$ (1 cup) was split into three equal parts of $5/15$ each. Thus, $2/3$ of a cup $(1/3 + 1/3)$ is equal to $10/15$ of a cup $(5/15 + 5/15)$.

The ability to build on the equality of two ratios (a proportion) to develop a set of infinitely many equivalent ratios is a hallmark of proportional reasoning. Proportional reasoning is complex and involves at least the three related aspects in Essential Understanding 7.

Essential Understanding 7

Proportional reasoning is complex and involves understanding that—
- *equivalent ratios can be created by iterating and/or partitioning a composed unit;*
- *if one quantity in a ratio is multiplied or divided by a particular factor, then the other quantity must be multiplied or divided by the same factor to maintain the proportional relationship; and*
- *the two types of ratios—composed units and multiplicative comparisons—are related.*

The idea of forming a ratio as a composed unit is a foundational concept that is not, by itself, indicative of sophisticated ratio reasoning. In fact, some researchers refer to the formation of a composed unit as *pre-ratio* reasoning (Lesh, Post, and Behr 1988). Essential Understanding 7 presents three crucial aspects of sophisticated proportional reasoning. These three components are presented in order of increasing sophistication, although not everyone comes to an understanding of them in this particular order. The discussion that follows is an introduction to these ideas; a full development of them is beyond the scope of this book.

Creating equivalent ratios

At the beginning levels of proportional reasoning, students iterate (repeat) and/or partition (break into equal-sized parts) a composed unit to create a family of equivalent ratios. For example, consider the following problem:

> Begin with a ramp that is 3 centimeters high and has a base that is 4 centimeters long. Make all the ramps you can that have the same steepness as the original ramp but are not identical to it.

If a student makes a copy of the original ramp, then both ramps have the same steepness, since neither the height nor the length of the base changed (see fig. 1.26). Aligning the ramp and its copy "tip to tip," as shown in figure 1.27, will not change the steepness of either ramp. The resulting ramp, with a height of 6 centimeters

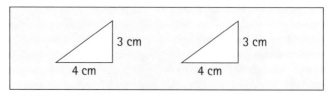

Fig. 1.26. A ramp and an identical copy of it

and a base of 8 centimeters, has the same steepness as the original ramp. The iteration process can be continued to create other ramps with the same steepness: a ramp with a height of 12 centimeters and a base of 16 centimeters, one with a height of 21 centimeters and a base of 28 centimeters, and so forth.

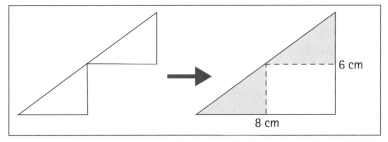

Fig. 1.27. A new ramp with the same steepness as the original, made by aligning the original and its copy tip to tip (dotted lines complete the drawing of the new ramp)

Students can also partition the original ramp to form new ramps of equal steepness. Partitioning the height of the original ramp into two equal parts and partitioning the base into two equal parts results in a new ramp with a height of $1^1/_2$ centimeters and a base of 2 centimeters (see fig. 1.28). Students can verify that the new ramp has the same steepness as the original ramp by iterating the new ramp and stacking as before to obtain the original ramp. They can use partitioning to create additional ramps with the same steepness. For example, partitioning the height and base of the original ramp into thirds results in a new ramp with a height of 1 centimeter and a base of $1^1/_3$ centimeters.

Fig. 1.28. Partitioning a ramp to form a new ramp with the same steepness

Students can combine iterating and partitioning. For example, suppose students are asked to determine the height of a new ramp with a base of 5 centimeters and the same steepness as the original 3 : 4 ramp. This is a much harder problem for students because of the relatively small difference between 4 and 5 centimeters. However, they can combine partitioning and iterating to tackle this problem.

Consider the thinking of one middle school student, Marco. He realized that the base of the new ramp was 1 centimeter more than the base of the original ramp, so he decided to find the height of a ramp that had a base of 1 centimeter and the same steepness as the original ramp. He partitioned the $3:4$ original ramp into 4 equal parts to obtain a $3/4 : 1$ ramp. He then iterated and stacked the $3/4 : 1$ ramp five times so that the base of the new ramp was 5 centimeters. The height new ramp was $15/4$, or $33/4$, centimeters, since it contained five ramps, each with a height of $3/4$ centimeter.

Maintaining a proportional relationship

An important part of developing more sophisticated proportional reasoning is the ability to truncate the work of iterating a composed unit by using the arithmetic operation of multiplication. To accomplish this, students need to move from simply repeating a composed unit multiple times until they reach a particular goal to being able to anticipate the number of groups that they need.

Consider the work of a middle school student, Andrea. She needed to determine the base of a ramp with a height of 27 centimeters and the same steepness as the original ramp—again, the ramp with a height of 3 centimeters and a base of 4 centimeters. Andrea began by drawing a picture of four stacked ramps like the original. She determined the height of the resulting new ramp by adding the heights of the stacked ramps ($3 + 3 + 3 + 3 = 12$ centimeters). Andrea realized that she had not used enough copies of the original ramp. She then added another to the stack and again added to determine the height of the new ramp ($3 + 3 + 3 + 3 + 3 = 15$ centimeters). Andrea continued this process until she drew a new ramp with a height of 27 centimeters and a base of 36 centimeters. Although she eventually arrived at a correct response, her reasoning had not achieved the sophistication demonstrated by David's response, discussed below.

David approached the problem by imagining the height of the new ramp (27 centimeters) as made up of 9 groups of 3 centimeters. As a result, David could conceive of multiplying the height of the original ramp by 9 (3 centimeters $\times$ 9 = 27 centimeters). Because David recognized that he needed to iterate the entire $3:4$ ramp 9 times, he knew that he should also multiply the base by 9 (4 centimeters $\times$ 9 = 36 centimeters).

David's work is consistent with understanding that multiplication can abbreviate the longer process of repeated iteration. For students like Andrea, a critical part of developing this understanding is to have repeated experiences that prompt them to reflect on the number of groups that they have formed as a result of iterating. For example, Andrea was able to solve the problem through repeated iteration and counting. She may have been unaware that she used nine copies of the original ramp to create the new ramp. Asking students to reflect on the number of groups (in this instance, ramps) that they used is a critical part of their eventually becoming able to anticipate the number of groups that they need.

It is possible to generalize the understanding reflected in David's work: If one quantity is multiplied by a particular factor, then the other quantity must also be multiplied by the same factor to maintain the proportional relationship. Similarly, if one quantity is divided by a factor, then the other quantity must be divided by the same factor to maintain the proportional relationship. To achieve this understanding, students need to link the act of partitioning to the operation of division and develop an awareness of the number of parts that they create when they partition repeatedly.

For example, suppose that a student needs to determine the base of a ramp that has a height of 1 centimeter and the same steepness as the original $3:4$ ramp. By imagining 3 centimeters as composed of 3 groups of 1 centimeter, the student can conceive of partitioning the height of the original ramp into 3 equal groups. By linking partitioning with the arithmetic operation of division, the student can obtain the desired height by dividing 3 centimeters by 3 to get 1 centimeter. Because the height is divided by 3, the base must also be divided by 3, and 4 centimeters $\div$ 3 is $4/3$, or $1\frac{1}{3}$, centimeters. Thus, a ramp with a height of 1 centimeter and a base of $1\frac{1}{3}$ centimeters will have the same steepness as the ramp with a height of 3 centimeters and a base of 4 centimeters. Dividing each quantity (the height and the base) by the same factor, 3, can also be thought of as multiplying each quantity by a factor of $1/3$. In fact, understanding that maintaining a proportional relationship involves multiplying each quantity by the same factor can be extended to include fractional factors.

Reconsider Marco's reasoning, presented previously. Marco needed to find the height of a ramp with a base of 5 centimeters and the same steepness as the original $3:4$ ramp. Marco partitioned the $3:4$ ramp into 4 equal parts to obtain a $3/4:1$ ramp. He then iterated and stacked the $3/4:1$ ramp five times so that the base of the new ramp was 5 centimeters. As a result, the height of the new ramp was $15/4$, or $3\frac{3}{4}$, centimeters, since it contained five ramps, each with a height of $3/4$ centimeters.

Eventually, Marco should develop his thinking to understand the use of fractional factors in such a context. For example, he could begin by realizing that 5 centimeters (the base of the new ramp) is $5/4$ of 4 centimeters (the base of the original ramp). Identifying the factor $5/4$ can grow out of Marco's reflection on his use of iterating and partitioning. Marco found $1/4$ of 4 centimeters by partitioning 4 centimeters into 4 equal parts. Conceptually, this work is the same as finding $1/4 \times 4$ centimeters. Then Marco iterated the result 5 times. This activity is the same conceptually as taking 5 one-fourths of 4 centimeters, which is $5/4 \times 4$ centimeters.

Once a student realizes that 5 centimeters is $5/4 \times 4$ centimeters, he or she can complete the problem by finding $5/4 \times 3$ centimeters, which is $15/4$, or $3 3/4$, centimeters. In sum, students like Marco are close to realizing that they can maintain a proportional relationship by multiplying each quantity by the same factor a/b.

Relating the two types of ratios

The discussion thus far has focused on proportional reasoning strategies that rely on thinking of ratios as composed units, because this is usually the easier entry point for middle school students. However, it is also important that students learn to work with multiplicative comparisons and connect these two types of ratios. For example, consider the set of heights and lengths (bases) of all of the equally steep ramps that have been discussed so far in relation to Essential Understanding 7 (see fig. 1.29).

Height (cm)	Length of Base (cm)
3	4
6	8
9	12
12	16
21	28
27	36
1.5	2
$3/4$	1
1	$4/3$
$3 3/4$	5

Fig. 1.29. Heights and lengths (bases) for a set of equally steep ramps (with shaded rows showing the unit ratios)

In each case, the height is $3/4$ of the length of the base, and the length of the base is $4/3$ times the height. These two ratios, $3/4$ and $4/3$, are multiplicative comparisons. To form the ratio $3/4$, students can ask, "What part of the length of the base is the height?" To form the ratio $4/3$, they can ask, "How many times greater is the length of the base than its height?" Using multiplicative comparisons is a powerful proportional reasoning strategy. For example, to find the length of the base of a ramp that has a height of 16 centimeters and the same steepness as the original $3:4$ ramp, students can simply multiply the height by $4/3$ (16 centimeters $\times 4/3 = 21 1/3$

centimeters). Similarly, if they have the length of the base of a ramp of this steepness, they can find the height of the ramp simply by multiplying the base by $3/4$.

It is important for students to connect composed units with multiplicative comparisons. Perhaps the easiest way for them to see the connection is by looking at either of the unit ratios (shown in the shaded rows in fig. 1.29). Consider the connections made by Manuel, a seventh grader. Manuel formed a composed unit of 1 centimeter (height) and $4/3$ centimeter (length of the base). He iterated the $1:4/3$ ramp to form other ramps of equal steepness. By iterating $1:4/3$ twice, he obtained a ramp with a height of 2 centimeters and a base of $2 2/3$ centimeters. By iterating $1:4/3$ three times, he found a ramp with a height of 3 centimeters and a base of 4 centimeters. When asked for the length of the base of a ramp with a height of 8 centimeters, Manuel reasoned that a height of 8 centimeters was made up of eight groups of 1 centimeter. For each 1 centimeter of height, he needed $4/3$ centimeters in the base. Because he needed eight groups of $4/3$ centimeters for the base, he multiplied $8 \times 4/3$. Manuel went on to find the bases of other ramps of equal steepness by multiplying the given heights by $4/3$.

Manuel appeared to understand that the base of each of these equally steep ramps was $4/3$ times as great as its height. This suggests that he formed a multiplicative comparison between the bases and heights of the ramps by expanding on his initial use of composed units. This connection between multiplicative comparisons and composed units allowed Manuel to write an equation to represent the relationship between the height and base of any ramp in this "same steepness" family. Specifically, Manuel wrote $H \times 4/3 = L$ and explained that could find any length (L) of the base of any ramp by multiplying its height (H) by $4/3$.

Essential Understanding 8

A rate is a set of infinitely many equivalent ratios.

This chapter's discussion of the essential understandings related to the big idea of proportional reasoning has moved from the formation of a ratio to reasoning with two equivalent ratios (a proportion) to the formation of a set of equivalent ratios—a hallmark of proportional reasoning. It is important to draw attention to the development of a set of equivalent ratios because many textbook treatments stop with proportions (two equivalent ratios). As a result, instruction may leave students without being able to use reasoning—as opposed to using often poorly understood procedures—to form a collection of equivalent ratios. Another way to say that a student has formed a set of infinitely many equivalent ratios is to say that he or she has conceived of a *rate*.

Thompson (1994) advocates this unconventional use of the term *rate* to signify a set of infinitely many equivalent ratios. Two other meanings of *rate* are more common. *Rate* is often defined as a comparison of two quantities of different units (e.g., gallons of gas consumed to miles traveled), in contrast to *ratio*, which is often defined as a comparison of two quantities of like units (e.g., feet to feet). *Rate* also is commonly used to refer to a ratio in which one of the quantities is time (e.g., miles to hours).

Thompson argues that these definitions locate the distinction between ratio and rate in the *situation* rather than in the way that a student *conceives* of the situation. Furthermore, he argues that characterizing a ratio in terms of how one thinks about it (e.g., as a multiplicative comparison or as a composed unit) has the advantage of making the "same unit versus different unit" distinction unimportant.

In fact, this chapter has used contexts of both types interchangeably. In the ramp context, the units for both base and height were the same (e.g., centimeters), but in the speed context, the units for distance and time were different (e.g., centimeters and seconds). Moreover, Thompson's use of rate is more consistent with how rate is used in advanced mathematical topics. In calculus, the derivative of a function at a particular point is conceived as an instantaneous *rate* of change at that point; it does not matter whether the units of the two quantities related by the function are the same or not.

For teachers, characterizing rate in terms of one's thinking rather than in terms of features of a situation can provide useful language to assess differences in levels of sophistication in students' reasoning. Consider the problem in figure 1.30 about the ratio of orange concentrate to water in a "recipe" for orange juice.

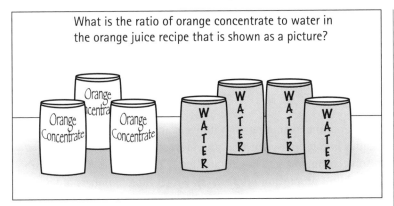

What is the ratio of orange concentrate to water in the orange juice recipe that is shown as a picture?

Fig. 1.30. A problem with a pictured "recipe" for orange juice

Suppose that a student writes "3 : 4." He or she could conceive of the situation in at least these three different ways:

1. *Not as a ratio.* The student may have counted 3 cans of orange concentrate and 4 cans of water by using only whole-number counting skills and then have written 3 : 4 or $4/3$ without forming a ratio conceptually.

2. *As a ratio.* The student may have formed a composed unit of 3 cans of orange concentrate and 4 cans of water and doubled the 3 : 4 unit to determine that a batch of orange juice made from 6 cans of orange concentrate and 8 cans of water would taste equally orangey. However, the student's reasoning may be limited to thinking about and finding easy equivalent ratios—for example, through doubling or halving.

3. *As a rate.* The student may be able to use proportional reasoning to determine the amount of orange concentrate and water for *any* quantity of orange juice of this strength. For example, the student may understand that he or she would need $5^1/_4$ cans of orange concentrate for 7 cans of water, 1 can of orange concentrate for $1^1/_3$ cans of water, $1/_3$ can of orange concentrate for $4/_9$ can of water, and so on.

Thinking about rate in this manner can help you guard against overestimating your students' proportional reasoning abilities. For example, students often show facility in reasoning with halves and doubles long before they are able to identify equivalent ratios by working with more difficult factors, such as $7/_8$ or $3/_5$. When you observe students forming "easy" ratios, you may be tempted to attribute more sophisticated proportional reasoning to them than is warranted. Making a distinction between ratio and rate can prompt you to assess your students' level of reasoning by posing problems that motivate them to form an extensive set of equivalent ratios, including ratios obtained by reasoning with more "difficult" numbers.

Essential Understanding 9

Several ways of reasoning, all grounded in sense making, can be generalized into algorithms for solving proportion problems

Using and understanding algorithms is an important part of mathematics because an algorithm provides a general and efficient way to solve an important class of problems. The most popular algorithm for tackling proportion problems in which three numbers are given and one is missing is the cross-multiplication algorithm. However, this algorithm is rarely grounded in sense making for students. In fact, sense making about the meaning of the quantities in a real-world setting is suspended in performing the cross-multiplication step of the algorithm.

Consider the following task:

The label on a box of cheese crackers tells consumers that 6 crackers contain 70 calories. How many calories are in 20 crackers?

Students can set up a proportion,

$$\frac{\text{Calories}}{\text{Crackers}} \quad \frac{70}{6} = \frac{x}{20}$$

and perform cross multiplication to arrive at the equation $6x = 70 \times 20$. However, the unit for the product 70 calories $\times$ 20 crackers has no meaning, because "calorie-cracker" does not make sense. The unit associated with 70×20 is not calories per cracker, which would be meaningful. Therefore, performing cross multiplication involves momentarily suspending sense making.

However, alternative solution methods maintain sense making and generalize for any values of the quantities. This section presents one such method, called the "unit ratio" method, and develops several associated understandings. In the cracker problem above, the ratio of calories to crackers is 70 to 6. Applying Essential Understanding 5, you can reinterpret the ratio 70:6 as the quotient $70 \div 6$, which is approximately 11.67 and represents the number of calories in one cracker. Because 20 crackers have 20 times as many calories as one cracker, they have approximately 20×11.67, or about 233, calories.

This alternative approach involves forming a *unit ratio*, which is the amount of a quantity per one of a second quantity (in this example, number of calories per one cracker). This approach is grounded in making sense of the quantities in the situation. But does this unit ratio method generalize to all numbers? Reflect 1.7 asks you to consider a different problem in the same context but with "messier" numbers.

 Essential Understanding 5

Ratios can be meaningfully reinterpreted as quotients.

Reflect 1.7

Suppose that 18 wheat crackers have 167 calories. How many calories are in 11 crackers? Solve the problem using the unit ratio approach.

Note that the unit ratio method still works. Because the problem asks for the number of calories in 11 wheat crackers, it is useful to find the number of calories in one cracker. The ratio of calories to crackers is 167 : 18. By applying Essential Understanding 5, you can reinterpret this ratio as a quotient: $167 \div 18$ gives the number of calories in one cracker, or about 9.3. Because each of the 11 crackers has about 9.3 calories, the total number of calories is approximately 11×9.3, or about 102, calories.

Students often need additional understanding when they tackle problems in which the missing value is in the second quantity—in this instance, the number of calories rather than the number of crackers. Consider the following problem:

If 6 cheese crackers provide 70 calories, how many crackers will provide 300 calories?

Students might start by dividing 70 by 6, in part because dividing the bigger number by the smaller number seems natural to them from their experiences in elementary school. However, the question asks for the number of crackers that someone needs to eat to get 300 calories. Consequently, students need to determine the number of crackers that one should eat to get just 1 calorie. Every 6 crackers provide 70 calories, a fact that the ratio 6 : 70 represents. Students who have grasped Essential Understanding 5 can reinterpret this ratio as $6 \div 70$ and understand that the quotient is the amount of crackers that yields one calorie, or approximately 0.086 of one cracker. Because someone has to eat about 0.086 of a cracker for each of 300 calories, the total number of crackers that he or she must eat is 300×0.086, or about 26 crackers.

Many other ways to solve proportion problems are also grounded in sense making. The goal of this section was to illustrate one generalizable alternative to the cross-multiplication algorithm that preserves sense making. However, before students attempt to apply proportional reasoning in any problem context, they need to be able to decide whether or not the quantities in the situation are in fact related proportionally. Being able to make this determination depends on understanding the important notion developed in Essential Understanding 10.

Essential Understanding 10

Superficial cues present in the context of a problem do not provide sufficient evidence of proportional relationships between quantities.

Problem solvers should base their decision to use proportional reasoning on the nature of the quantities in a particular situation. Too often, however, students rely on the following types of superficial cues to decide whether or not a situation involves a proportion:

- The problem gives 3 numbers, and 1 other number is missing.

- The problem involves key words such as *per*, *rate*, or *speed*.

- The problem appears in a chapter on ratios and proportions.

The following tasks (Lamon 1999, p. 223) illustrate these points:

1. If one football player weighs 225 pounds, then how much will three players weigh?

2. One man can paint the bedroom by himself in 3 hours. How long will it take two men to paint the room if both men paint at the same pace?

3. Bob and Marty run laps together because they both run at the same speed. Today, Marty started running before Bob came out of the locker room. Marty had run 6 laps by the time Bob ran 3. How many laps had Marty run by the time Bob had run 12?

4. You put a bucket under a dripping faucet. The bucket had 6 ounces in it to begin with. You come back after 8 minutes and notice that there are now 10 ounces in the bucket. How many ounces will be in the bucket after 17 minutes?

If students think that they should set up a proportion whenever three numbers are given and one is missing, then they are likely to set up a proportion for problem 1:

$$\frac{1}{225} = \frac{3}{x}.$$

Solving for x yields 675 lbs. However, the goal is for students to use their common sense about the real world *before* operating with the numbers. In this case, it is unlikely that every football player weighs 225 pounds. It would be more reasonable to find the weight of each player and add all the weights together. The situation would call for proportional reasoning if the problem stated that 225 pounds was an average weight for the football players and called for an approximation of the total weight of three players.

The strategy of setting up a proportion whenever the statement of a task gives three numbers and a fourth number is missing is even more problematic in the case of problem 2. Setting up the proportion

$$\frac{1}{3} = \frac{2}{x}$$

leads to an incorrect response of 6 hours. In a proportional situation, two quantities increase (or decrease) together at the same rate. To determine if this is happening in a particular situation, problem solvers can usefully consider what happens when one quantity increases. In the situation in problem 2, if more people arrive to paint, it will actually take *less* time—not more—to paint the room. Thus, the relationship between the number of workers and the amount of time it takes to paint the room is not directly proportional.

Without considering the details of a situation, students sometimes set up a proportion when they see terms such as *per*, *rate*, or *speed* in a problem statement. In problem 3, students might set up a proportion such as

$$\frac{6}{x} = \frac{3}{12},$$

leading them to find, incorrectly, that Marty would have completed 24 laps.

When two quantities are related proportionally, they are in a "many-to-one" relationship that holds across values. For example, consider the following proportional situation:

If 2 bags of topsoil weigh 30 pounds, how much will 3 of these bags weigh?

In this situation, each bag weighs 15 pounds, and this relationship continues for any number of bags. The running context also has a "many-to-one" relationship: You can think about Marty as having run 2 laps for each lap that Bob ran up to the time when Marty had completed 6 laps because 6 = 2 × 3. However, this relationship does not continue. When Marty runs one more lap, so does Bob, because Marty and Bob are running at the same speed. Consequently, when Marty has run 7 laps, Bob will have run 4 laps (and 7 is not 2 × 4). Note that this situation is additive in nature. Once Bob has run 3 laps, he needs to run 9 more to complete 12 laps. Therefore, Marty will have run 6 + 9, or 15, laps when Bob has run 12.

Finally, if problem 4 appeared in a chapter on proportional reasoning, some students would inappropriately set up the proportion

$$\frac{8}{10} = \frac{17}{x}$$

in an attempt to solve it. One way to determine whether or not quantities are related proportionally is to explore whether doubling both quantities results in the relationship remaining constant. In this case, if the time doubles, the water level in the cup does not double, because the bucket held some water to start. Thus, the water level and the elapsed time are not in a proportional relationship. However, a proportional relationship does hold between the *change* in the water level and the *change* in the time, as chapter 2 will discuss.

Conclusion

Proportional reasoning is a milestone in students' cognitive development. An understanding of proportionality develops slowly over a number of years. Yet, maturation alone does not ensure the development of proportional reasoning. Many adults in our society do not reason proportionally. The complexity of proportional reasoning is highlighted by the fact that the ability to execute the cross-multiplication algorithm correctly does not ensure the ability to reason proportionally. Furthermore, one who can reason effectively with doubles and halves may be unable to reason proportionally with more difficult numbers.

Reasoning proportionally involves many understandings, including grasping the meaning of a ratio as a multiplicative comparison and as a composed unit; making connections among ratios, fractions, and quotients; and understanding the ideas involved in moving from basic to more sophisticated levels of proportional reasoning. Because proportional reasoning is complex, developing the big idea and the associated understandings is not easy. It involves deepening your own understanding as a teacher, being sensitive to the types of reasoning that are most accessible as entry points for your students while pushing them to develop more sophisticated forms of reasoning, and being aware of typical shifts in students' learning of these ideas. Chapter 3 will address issues of teaching, learning, and assessment, but first chapter 2 will make connections between the essential understandings of proportional reasoning and other mathematical content. Specifically, chapter 2 will show how these ideas support a richer exploration of high school content and what concepts are critical for students to have developed in elementary school as prerequisites for the development of proportional reasoning in grades 6–8.

Connections: Looking Back and Ahead in Learning

Tʜɪs chapter considers how teachers can use the essential understandings associated with the big idea of ratios, proportions, and proportional reasoning to deepen their understanding of upper middle school and high school mathematics content related to slope, linear functions, and algebraic equations. It then briefly discusses the idea that proportional reasoning is at the heart of what it means to understand measurement across grade levels. Finally, it identifies several foundational ideas related to fractions and multiplication that elementary school teachers should address because they are critical to students' development of proportional reasoning.

Using the Essential Understandings to Reason about Linear Functions, Algebraic Equations, and Slope

Teachers who understand the big idea of proportional reasoning developed in chapter 1 can draw on the various related essential understandings to see familiar concepts in new ways. Consider some of the important sense making that can occur when teachers apply this new understanding to linear functions, algebraic equations, and the concept of slope.

Linear functions of the form $y = mx$

Upper middle school and high school students need to understand that a linear expression of the form $y = mx$ is a statement of proportionality, with m as an invariant ratio, also called the *constant of proportionality*. Karplus, Pulos, and Stage (1983) characterized *proportional reasoning* as "a term that denotes reasoning in a system of two variables between which there exists a linear functional relationship" (p. 219).

49

Returning to the speed context involving the clown and frog presented in chapter 1 can help flesh out the connection between proportionality and linearity. Recall that students in one class were shown a computer screen with SimCalc Mathworlds software showing two characters—a clown and a frog—with the clown set to walk 10 centimeters in 4 seconds (see p. 16). Suppose that students have used the types of reasoning articulated in chapter 1 to generate distance and time pairs that represent the same speed as walking 10 centimeters in 4 seconds. The graph of these data, shown in figure 2.1, represents infinitely many pairs of time and distance values that express the same speed of 2.5 cm/sec. Students can represent the distance and time pairs from the table in the figure as a set of ordered pairs: {(4, 10), (8, 20), (12, 30), (2, 5), (6, 15), (1, 2.5), (3, 7.5), (5, 12.5), (2.5, 6.25), (0.4, 1), (4.3, 10.75)}. They can conceive of the ordered pairs, in turn, as ratios, applying the idea in Essential Understanding 2. They can form ratios as multiplicative comparisons by considering how many times greater each y-value is than the corresponding x-value. For example, in the ordered pair (4, 10), 10 is 2.5 times greater than 4.

➡️ **Essential Understanding 2**

A ratio is a multiplicative comparison of two quantities, or it is a joining of two quantities in a composed unit.

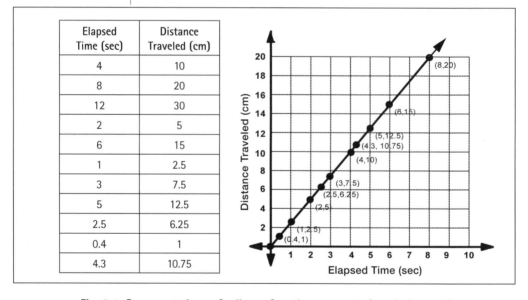

Fig. 2.1. Representations of a linear function as a set of equivalent ratios

Alternatively, students can form ratios as composed units. For example, if they form a composed unit from the ordered pair (2, 5), they can generate other ordered pairs in the set by operating on 2:5. For instance, they can obtain the ratio represented by the point (2.5, 6.25) by partitioning the composed unit 2:5 into four equal parts, and they can conceive of each part as the composed unit 0.5:1.25. They can then combine the two ratios 0.5:1.25 and 2:5 to arrive at the ratio 2.5 : 6.25, which they can represent by the point (2.5, 6.25). Thus, they can also conceive of the set of ordered pairs representing the same speed as an infinite set of equivalent ratios:

$$\frac{10}{4} = \frac{20}{8} = \frac{30}{12} = \frac{5}{2} = \frac{15}{6} = \frac{2.5}{1} = 2.5 = \frac{7.5}{3} = \frac{12.5}{5} = \frac{6.25}{2.5} = \frac{1}{0.4} = \frac{10.75}{4.3} = \ldots$$

Algebraic equations

Another way for students to see the connection between linearity and proportionality is by forming an equation that relates time and distance values—namely, $y = 2.5x$, where x represents the elapsed time and y represents the distance traveled. Isolating 2.5 algebraically by dividing each side by x yields $y/x = 2.5$. Students who are developing important understanding related to ratios, proportions, and proportional reasoning will realize that this equation represents the set of equivalent ratios shown above—namely, the set of ratios such that each ratio of the y-value to its corresponding x-value is equivalent to 2.5.

The equation $y = 2.5x$ can also be interpreted *directly* in terms of ratios. One interpretation is that each y-value is 2.5 times as great as its corresponding x-value. Interpreting the equation in this way is the same as forming a ratio as a multiplicative comparison of y-values to corresponding x-values. A second interpretation of the equation $y = 2.5x$ involves seeing 2.5 as the number of centimeters that the clown travels in a second. Then the total distance traveled is 2.5 centimeters for each second that passes as the clown travels. For example, the ordered pair (6, 15) means that after 6 seconds, the clown has traveled 2.5 centimeters for each of 6 seconds, which is represented by $2.5 \times 6 = 15$. Students can develop this interpretation from reasoning with composed units. For example, partitioning the original composed unit of 10 : 4 into four equal parts yields 2.5 centimeters in 1 second for each part. Iterating 2.5 : 1 six times yields 15 centimeters in 6 seconds. The connection between proportionality and linearity emphasizes *covariation*; the quantities of distance and time change continuously and simultaneously while preserving the invariant ratio of 2.5 cm/sec.

Linear functions of the form *y = mx + b*

Any linear function can be expressed in the form $y = mx + b$. Furthermore, $y = mx + b$ is a statement of proportionality, represented by $y = mx$, combined with a vertical translation, represented by the addition of b. To help you consider the development of this idea in the context of speed, Reflect 2.1 introduces a situation in which a rabbit is already a certain distance from home when it begins walking.

Reflect 2.1

Suppose a rabbit is 4 centimeters from home when it begins walking, and after 3 seconds it is 11.5 centimeters from home. Generate several "distance from home" and elapsed time values for other parts of the rabbit's journey so that the rabbit travels the same speed throughout its journey.

One way to approach this situation is to consider the distance that the rabbit travels in the first 3 seconds. This distance is the difference between the rabbit's distance from home after 3 seconds and its initial distance from home—namely, 11.5 – 4, or 7.5, centimeters. To determine the rabbit's speed, you can form a composed unit of the distance traveled to the elapsed time, or 7.5:3. You can find the number of centimeters traveled in 1 second by partitioning 7.5:3 into 3 equal parts. Splitting 7.5 centimeters into 3 equal parts gives 2.5 centimeters in each part, and splitting 3 seconds into 3 equal parts gives 1 second in each part. Thus, the rabbit travels 2.5 centimeters in 1 second. You can use this unit ratio to determine how far the rabbit is from home over time. After 4 seconds, it is an additional 2.5 centimeters from home, or 11.5 + 2.5, or 14, centimeters from home, as figure 2.2 shows.

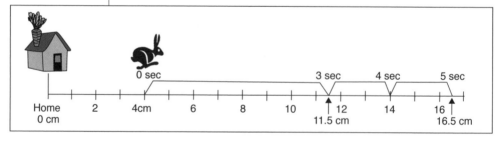

Fig. 2.2. A rabbit begins walking 4 centimeters from home and maintains a constant speed.

Continuing in this manner enables you to produce a table of values such as that shown in figure 2.3. The figure shows a graph of these values (line B) on the same Cartesian grid as the graph of $y = 2.5x$ (line A), which shows the distance and time the distance and time values for the clown's walking in the earlier situation. Showing the graphs together highlights important connections and differences between the two functions. First, line B is a vertical translation of line A by 4 units. Hence, because the equation for line A is $y = 2.5x$, the equation for line B is $y = 2.5x + 4$. For any given x-value, the corresponding y-value for line B is 4 greater than the y-value for line A. For instance, when $x = 4$ (in other words, 4 seconds have passed), the rabbit in the situation represented by line A has traveled 10 centimeters ($4 \times 2.5 = 10$) and is 10 centimeters from home. After 4 seconds, the rabbit in the situation represented by line B has also traveled 10 cm (4×2.5) but is 14 centimeters from home ($4 \times 2.5 + 4$).

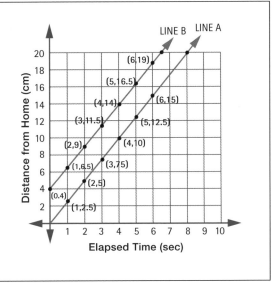

Elapsed Time (sec)	Distance from Home (cm)
0	4
3	11.5
1	6.5
4	14
5	16.5
6	19
2	9
8	24
2.5	10.25

Fig. 2.3. A table and a corresponding graph (line B) for a rabbit that starts walking 4 centimeters from home and maintains a constant speed

Examining the graphs helps to point out a second important difference between the two functions. The relationship represented by line A is proportional, but the relationship represented by line B is not. Specifically, you can apply Essential Understanding 7 from chapter 1 to see that any two ordered pairs on line A are related by some factor a/b. For example, the ordered pairs (8, 20) and (4, 10) on line A are related by a factor of 2. Both x- and y-coordinates of the point (8, 20) on line A are double the corresponding coordinates for (4, 10). This doubling relationship does not hold for the points on line B. For example, the x-coordinate of (8, 24) is double the x-coordinate of (4, 14), but the y-coordinates do not show this relationship: 24 is not double 14.

Finally, you can see every point on line A as representing the rabbit's speed simply by forming a ratio of the y- value to its corresponding x-value. You cannot do this in the case of line B, where you need two points to determine the rabbit's speed. The next section, on slope, elaborates this point.

Slope

The slope of a function is the rate of change in one quantity relative to the change of another quantity, where the two quantities related by the function covary. Recall that Essential Understanding 8 expresses a *rate* as a set of equivalent ratios. The slope formula is typically expressed as

$$m = \frac{y_2 - y_1}{x_2 - x_1}$$

Essential Understanding 7

Proportional reasoning is complex and involves understanding that—
- *equivalent ratios can be created by iterating and/ or partitioning a composed unit;*
- *if one quantity in a ratio is multiplied or divided by a particular factor, then the other quantity must be multiplied or divided by the same factor to maintain the proportional relationship; and*
- *the two types of ratios—composed units and multiplicative comparisons—are related.*

➡️ Essential
Understanding 8

*A rate is a set of
infinitely many
equivalent ratios.*

for any two points (x_1, y_1) and (x_2, y_2) on the line, or, more colloqui-
ally, as

$$m = \frac{rise}{run}.$$

However, it is not necessary to use the slope formula to determine the slope of a line of the form $y = mx$. For example, you can
find the slope of line A in figure 2.3 by forming a ratio of the y-val-
ue to its corresponding x-value for any point on the line. You can
use the point (4, 10) to form the ratio 10:4, or $^{10}/_4$; you can use the
point (8, 20) to form the ratio 20:8, or $^{20}/_8$; and so on, producing a
set of equivalent ratios. Although the conventional representation
of the slope of this function is 2.5, any member of the set can represent the slope, since all values are equivalent. In fact, you can think
of line A itself as representing the slope, since the slope of the line
is a set of infinitely many equivalent ratios—that is, slope is a rate.

Finding differences of x- and y-values as the slope formula
directs is necessary only for lines of the form $y = mx + b$. Consider
how informal reasoning about the rabbit's walking situation, mod-
eled by line B in figure 2.3, connects with the slope formula. In
this "head start" situation, the slope of the function is a measure of
the rabbit's speed. Speed is a ratio of distance traveled to the corresponding amount of time elapsed. Select any two points on the
graph of line B—say, (4, 14) and (6, 19). The first point indicates
that the rabbit was 14 centimeters from home after 4 seconds; the
second point indicates that it was 19 centimeters from home after 6
seconds. The elapsed time is 6 – 4, or 2, seconds. During these
two seconds, the rabbit traveled 19 – 14, or 5, centimeters. Thus,
the rabbit's speed is the ratio 5 centimeters to 2 seconds, which is
equivalent to 2.5 cm/sec. This sensible informal approach can be
seen as an application of the slope formula:

$$m = \frac{y_2 - y_1}{x_2 - x_1} = \frac{(19 - 14) \text{ cm}}{(6 - 4) \text{ sec}} = \frac{5 \text{ cm}}{2 \text{ sec}} = 2.5 \text{ cm/sec}$$

Contrasting examples briefly show two students' reasoning
about slope when one of them does and the other does not connect linearity and proportionality. Chanise and Hector, both seventh
graders, had been working with a context in which water was being
pumped into a swimming pool. After having made sense of the context, they were shown the graph in figure 2.4. The graph indicates
that the pool held 6 gallons of water after 3 minutes, 10 gallons
after 5 minutes, and 18 gallons after 9 minutes. The students were
asked to find the slope of the line. Chanise correctly recorded the
slope formula as

$$m = \frac{rise}{run}.$$

She then drew a "stair step" beneath the line, connecting the
points (0, 0) and (3, 6). However, Chanise ignored the water and time

quantities when determining the "rise" and "run." Specifically, she counted 3 boxes along the base of the stair step and 2 boxes along the side of the stair step and recorded the slope as $2/3$. Chanise repeated this procedure, using the points $(3, 6)$ and $(5, 10)$. She found the run by counting 2 boxes along the base of her second stair step, and she apparently determined the rise by rounding the number of boxes along the side of the stair step to 1 box. She recorded a second slope of $1/2$. Chanise expressed frustration that the slope didn't work "because it has different amounts on the sides and the rise and the runs," and she concluded that the slope for this line changed. When asked to draw a line with a slope that did not change, Chanise plotted a point on the graph, went up 4 and over 2, plotted a new point, went up 4 and over 2, plotted a point, and then connected the points. This process suggests that she did not connect linearity and proportionality. Instead, she apparently associated slope with the idea of stairs of identical size rather than with a ratio that is invariant despite changes in particular "rise" and "run" values.

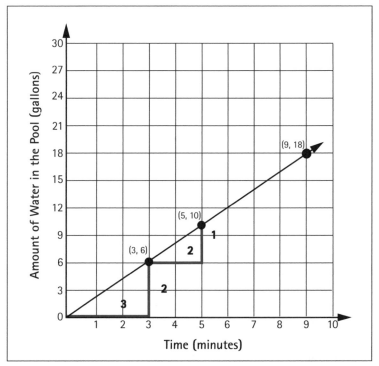

Fig. 2.4. Authors' illustration of one student's work to determine the slope of a line

In contrast, Hector correctly responded that the slope is 2. Although Hector had not yet been taught the slope formula, he was able to reason appropriately about slope by thinking about the relationship between the amount of water that had been pumped into the pool and the elapsed time, as indicated by the points on the graph. For example, when asked to write an equation, Hector wrote T × 2 = G, explaining that multiplying the time by 2 gives the number of gallons of water. When asked about the meaning of the 2, he replied that the 2 "would represent the speed…, or like how much you would get for every, for every 1 minute there would be like 2 gallons." He then used the equation to predict, correctly, the amount of water in the pool after 19 minutes, after 1 hour, and after 6.5 minutes. Hector's reasoning suggests a focus on a relationship between the amount of water and the elapsed time, reflecting both an interpretation of slope as a measure of how fast the pump is pumping and some sense of the invariance of the pumping rate of 2 gallons per minute.

Grounding Measurement in Proportional Reasoning

Proportional reasoning is central to an understanding of measurement (Lehrer 2003). Thompson and Saldanha (2003) point to the importance of conceiving of a measure as a ratio comparison rather than as a "number of things." An illustration of a measure as a "number of things" is thinking of 3 inches as three little "lengths," called "inches." In contrast, conceiving of a measure as a ratio comparison involves thinking of 3 inches as 3 times the length of 1 inch.

The formation of a multiplicative comparison between the length of the object to be measured and the particular standard of measurement is critical in situations in which the measurement unit changes. Suppose that you measure the height of a man as 6 feet. As a ratio comparison, the man's height is 6 times a 1-foot unit. If you change the unit that you use to measure the man's height from feet to inches, then you must recognize that the ratio of 1 foot to 1 inch is 12 : 1 (i.e., one foot is 12 times greater than 1 inch), and that this ratio is invariant across the change in measurement units. Because the man's height is 6 times greater than 1 foot, and 1 foot is 12 times greater than 1 inch, the height of the man is 6 × 12, or 72, times greater than 1 inch. Thus, the man's height is 72 inches.

This way of thinking about measurement is proportional in nature. In contrast, Thompson (1994) recounts a fifth grader's response to the question of whether the speed of a car could be measured in miles per century. The student responded, "No, because you would die, or the car would rust away before a century" (p. 179). The student's reply suggests that he or she confused the thing to be measured with its measurement and did not conceive of measure as a ratio comparison.

Foundations of Proportional Reasoning in the Elementary Grades

When work in elementary school allows students to develop deep and flexible meanings for numbers and operations (especially for fractions and multiplication), they have important foundations on which to build an understanding of ratios, proportions, and proportional reasoning in the middle grades.

Building on the meaning of fractions

As a prerequisite for developing proportional reasoning, students need to be able to conceive of a fraction such as $2/3$ as "2 one-thirds." Stated generally, the fraction a/b is "a one-$b$ths." However, elementary school students often learn to think of a fraction such as $2/3$ only as "2 parts *out* of 3 parts." When students have only an "out of" conception of fractions, they often have difficulty interpreting improper fractions. For example, they may claim that $4/3$ doesn't make sense, because "you can't have four things out of three." In contrast, if $4/3$ means "4 one-thirds," then it does make sense, because someone can have any number of one-thirds. For example, someone who has 6 one-thirds can group 3 one-thirds together twice, making two wholes.

Interpreting the fraction a/b as "a one-$b$ths" rather than as "a out of b" is central to forming a ratio as a multiplicative comparison. For example, forming a multiplicative comparison of 7 to 3 entails determining how many times greater 7 is than 3. Because this is a difficult comparison, think instead about comparing 7 to 1. Obviously 7 is 7 times greater than 1. However, 1 is also $1/3$ of 3 (see fig. 2.5). Thus, 7 is 7 times greater than $1/3$ of 3. To restate, 7 is 7 one-thirds of 3. This is the same as saying that 7 is $7/3$ of 3, since $7/3$ means 7 one-thirds. In sum, one way to form a multiplicative comparison between 7 and 3 (i.e., to reason that 7 is $7/3$ times greater than 3) relies on an understanding of $7/3$ as 7 one-thirds.

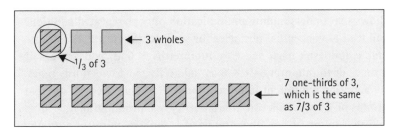

Fig. 2.5. Interpreting $7/3$ as 7 one-thirds to show that 7 is $7/3$ of 3

Prerequisite fraction knowledge supports students' understanding of another essential understanding of proportionality—namely,

➡️ Essential
Understanding 6

A proportion is a relationship of equality between two ratios. In a proportion, the ratio of two quantities remains constant as the corresponding values of the quantities change.

Essential Understanding 6, which indicates that a proportion is a relationship of equality between two ratios. In other words, something is invariant in a proportional relationship. Elementary school teachers can promote students' understanding of the idea of invariance by helping the students explore ways of representing a particular amount with different fractions. For example, consider the purple region in figure 2.6. You could name this region by at least three *different* fractions—as $1/4$ of 1, $1/8$ of 2, and $1/3$ of $3/4$—as illustrated in the figure. Thus, a fraction is not an amount; a fraction is a *relationship* or multiplicative comparison between two quantities. Furthermore, something is invariant across these three expressions: each represents the ratio of 1 to 4.

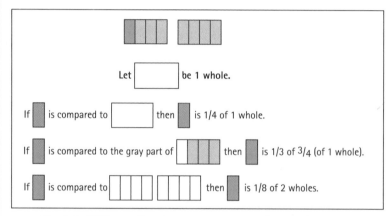

Fig. 2.6. Different fractions can represent the purple region.

Building on the meaning of multiplication

Just as certain conceptions of fractions are more powerful than others for proportional reasoning, particular ways of thinking about multiplication aid in the development of proportional reasoning. In particular, a conception of multiplication that extends beyond that of repeated addition is critical to proportional reasoning. If students interpret multiplication as repeated addition, then they will think that 5×6 means $6 + 6 + 6 + 6 + 6$, or "add 6 five times." Research shows that understanding multiplication only as repeated addition can lead to conceptual obstacles for students (Steffe 1994). For example, it doesn't make sense to interpret $1/2 \times 6$ as "add 6 one-half a time" or to interpret $5^2/_3 \times 6$ as "add 6 five and two-thirds times." By adopting a different interpretation of 5×6 as "five 6s" or "five groups of 6," students can interpret $5^2/_3 \times 6$ meaningfully as "five and two-thirds 6s," or "five groups of 6 and two-thirds of a group of 6." Five 6s is 30, and two-thirds of 6 is twice one-third of 6, which is twice 2, or 4. Therefore, $5^2/_3 \times 6 = 34$. This thinking is justified by the distributive property: $(5 + 2/_3) \times 6 = (5 \times 6) + (2/_3 \times 6)$.

The "groups of" conception of multiplication involves another important conceptual distinction from that of multiplication as repeated addition. In repeated addition, students deal only with units of one. In the "groups of" conception, multiplication involves the coordination of units of units (Clark and Kamii 1996), an activity that represents an important conceptual achievement for students. This thinking involves seeing proportionality in multiplication. For example, if students see 5 × 6 as repeated addition, they then combine units of one successively: 6 ones plus 6 more ones is 12 ones, plus 6 more ones gives 18 ones, and so on until 30 ones. In contrast, 5 × 6 can be conceived as 5 sixes (see fig. 2.7). At the top level are five units, each consisting of a six-unit. At the next level, a six-unit is a grouping that can be broken apart into six ones or packed back up again into one six. At the bottom level are the 30 ones.

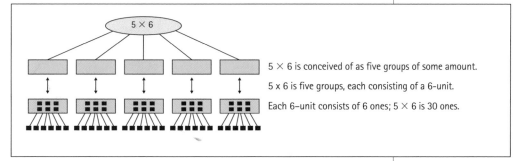

5 × 6 is conceived of as five groups of some amount.

5 x 6 is five groups, each consisting of a 6-unit.

Each 6–unit consists of 6 ones; 5 × 6 is 30 ones.

Fig. 2.7. The "groups of" interpretation of multiplication in the case of 5 × 6

The "groups of" conception of multiplication is important for proportional reasoning. In the case of 5 times a number p, for example, students can think of each of the 5 groups at the top level (as in fig. 2.7) with the groups being of any size. For example, 5 × 4 means 5 groups of 4; 5 × 2^3/$_7$ means 5 groups of 2^3/$_7$; and 5 × p means 5 groups of p. Students can interpret 5 × 6 as a quantity that is 5 times greater than 6. They can see that conversely, 6 is ^{1}/$_5$ of the product 5 × 6. Similarly, they can understand that 5p represents an amount that is 5 times greater than the amount represented by p and that p is ^{1}/$_5$ of the product 5p (Thompson and Saldanha 2003).

This thinking helps students interpret symbolic expressions in algebra. For example, they can interpret the linear function $y = 2.5x$ as follows: 2.5x represents an amount that is 2.5 times greater than the amount represented by x. This is a statement of proportional reasoning. Because y is equivalent to 2.5x, the "groups of" interpretation of multiplication allows students to form a ratio as a multiplicative comparison between corresponding y- and x-values.

Conclusion

Proportional reasoning is linked conceptually to a number of elementary, middle, and high school topics. Proportionality lies at the heart of understanding slope and linear functions, as well as measurement. Furthermore, reasoning proportionally depends on the meaning that one develops for numbers and operations in elementary school. This chapter has articulated the importance of interpreting a fraction a/b as a one-$b$ths and of understanding the "groups of" interpretation of multiplication. Both have implications for the development of proportional reasoning.

Chapter 3

Challenges: Learning, Teaching, and Assessing

THE development of proportional reasoning is an extended process that takes students through necessary transitions in their thinking. This chapter first discusses these steps in students' learning and suggests teaching approaches to help students through them. A comprehensive understanding of your students' path to proportional reasoning can allow you to build assessment into the process in a natural way. The remainder of the chapter discusses the role of assessment, detailing problem types and ways of assessing various levels of proportional reasoning.

Helping Students Make Transitions to Become Proportional Reasoners

Learning to reason proportionally happens slowly, over time. Students make multiple shifts in their thinking as they become increasingly adept at forming ratios, reasoning with proportions, and creating and understanding rates. The discussion that follows outlines four important transitions that students make as they develop proportional reasoning, and it details ways to negotiate these shifts and evaluate your students' current understanding.

Shift 1—From one quantity to two

Before students are able to reason with ratios, they typically focus on just one quantity. To help students make the crucial transition to realizing that they need to account for two quantities at the same time, you can introduce problems that motivate them to coordinate two quantities. Figure 3.1 shows an example of a complex quantitative situation (Ellis 2007) that calls on students to attend to two quantities in the process of isolating an attribute. Reflect 3.1 invites you to solve this problem for yourself.

Shift 1

Students need to make a transition from focusing on only one quantity to realizing that two quantities are important.

Connected Gears Problem

Say you have a small gear with 8 teeth connected to a
big gear with 12 teeth.

1. If the small gear turns clockwise, which direction does the big
   gear turn? Why?

2. If you turn the small gear a certain number of times, does the big
   gear turn more revolutions, fewer, or the same amount? How can
   you tell?

3. Find a way to keep track of how many revolutions the small gear
   makes. Find a way to keep track of how many revolutions the big
   gear makes. How can you keep track of both at the same time?

Fig. 3.1. A problem involving two connected gears

Reflect 3.1

Solve the Connected Gears problem in figure 3.1.

a. What attribute is involved in this problem?

b. What difficulties would you anticipate that your students would experience
with the problem?

Teaching Tip

*To help your students
make Shift 1, pose
problems that
motivate them to
isolate an attribute
in a complex
quantitative
situation.*

One group of seventh-grade students solved this problem by
working physically with gears (Ellis 2007). They quickly figured
out that the rotations of one gear depended on the rotations of the
other. Larissa explained, "Whenever this [the small gear] is spinning, this one [the big gear] has to be spinning, because this one
[the small gear] is in total control of the other one." The attribute
involved in this problem is often called the *gear ratio*. After finding answers to parts 1 and 2, the students decided to place a sticker
on one of the teeth of the big gear and another sticker on one of
the teeth of the small gear. The students lined up the stickers, and

rotated the gears until the stickers matched up again. This happened after the big gear had turned 2 times and the small gear had turned 3 times.

Shift 2—From additive to multiplicative comparisons

How the seventh graders in the example above compared the rotations of the two gears in the Connected Gears problem indicates whether they had made the second transition toward proportional reasoning. A student named Dani compared the rotations of the two gears in this way:

> If you count this one [the small gear], and it's gonna go 3 times, it's gonna go, let's see, 1, 2, 3. This one [the big gear], it's gonna end up, it's gonna meet again. This one's only gonna go 2 times, and this one's gonna go 3…. Or another way is you could do S − 1 = B.

In writing S − 1 = B, Dani made an additive comparison between the rotations of the two gears, instead of a multiplicative comparison. Comparing additively is natural for students who are not used to reasoning with ratios. In fact, the shift from additive reasoning to multiplicative reasoning is another important transition for students.

One way to help students make this transition from additive comparisons to ratios is to pose problems like the Connected Gears problem, which encourages them to take note of more than one instance of the same phenomenon. Furthermore, you can pose questions that motivate students to develop multiple ratios. In the classroom discussed above, the teacher anticipated that the students might compare the rotations additively and consequently prepared this follow-up question:

> You found out that when the small gear turns 3 times, the big gear turns 2 times. What are some other rotation pairs for the gears?

By assessing your students' current understanding and anticipating potential difficulties that they might experience, you can design tasks intended to help them develop a deeper understanding of proportional situations.

In response to the teacher's question, Dani and her classmates continued to rotate the gears. The students observed that the stickers matched up again when the big gear had turned 4 times and the small gear had turned 6 times, and again when the big gear had turned 6 times and the small gear had turned 9 times. Ultimately, they made a table like that shown in figure 3.2 to represent the rotation pairs for gear A (small) and gear B (big), beginning with the smallest pair (3, 2) and doubling it again and again.

Shift 2

Students need to make a transition from making an additive comparison to forming a ratio between two quantities.

 Teaching Tip

To help your students make Shift 2, gauge their current proportional reasoning and create appropriate learning situations that will help them develop more sophisticated understanding.

Gear A (Small)	Gear B (Big)
3	2
6	4
12	8
24	16
48	32
96	64
192	128

Fig. 3.2. Numbers of rotations necessary for tagged teeth in two gears to realign

As students make the transition from reasoning additively, they may at first create composed units rather than multiplicative comparisons. For example, when responding to the teacher's question about other rotation pairs for the gears, Dora offered this explanation:

> If you take, 'cause there's 8 teeth on one and 12 teeth on the other, you can just like go on forever and find the multiples of 8 and 12. If, you can get, the small one turns 3 and the big one turns 2, the small 6, the big 4, 12 and 8, 24 and 16, 48 and 32, 96 and 64, 192 and 128.

Dora joined two quantities—the 3 rotations of the small gear and the 2 rotations of the large gear—into the composed unit 3 : 2. She then iterated the 3 : 2 unit by multiplying both quantities by 2 to maintain the ratio relationship.

Consider another example of a problem that encourages students to begin to iterate in this way:

> The scale on a map indicates that 10 centimeters represents an actual distance of 4 miles. Find as many different map-distance and actual-distance pairs as you can.

Although doubling may be natural for many students, iterating or multiplying by other numbers may not be as easy. Likewise, students may need help in partitioning a composed unit into parts other than halves. You can ask questions that encourage students to create new composed units involving smaller numbers. For instance, suppose that a student who is working with the map scale in the problem has developed the composed unit 10 centimeters : 4 miles and can iterate that unit to create many other same-scale units, such as 20 centimeters and 8 miles, 50 centimeters and 20 miles, and so on. You could ask the student to find some same-scale pairs in which the numbers of centimeters and miles are smaller than in the original "10 centimeter : 4 mile" unit.

Another strategy for helping students expand their ability to partition a composed unit is to encourage them to draw pictures. For example, you could tell your students that 18 centimeters on a particular map represents an actual distance of 15 miles. You could ask the students to draw a picture to represent the unit "18 centimeters : 15 miles," as in figure 3.3, and then ask them to complete tasks (*a*) and (*b*) in the figure, showing $1/3$ of the journey, and giving the measurement of that distance, both on the map and in real life.

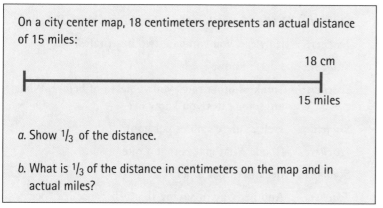

On a city center map, 18 centimeters represents an actual distance of 15 miles:

18 cm

15 miles

a. Show $1/3$ of the distance.

b. What is $1/3$ of the distance in centimeters on the map and in actual miles?

Fig. 3.3. A problem motivating students to partition a composed unit

It is easy to overestimate students' proportional reasoning abilities, especially if you assign problems with simple numbers. Students typically develop the ability to do basic iterating and partitioning, such as halving and doubling, early on. Although they may be able to solve simple introductory problems, they are likely to need additional practice with a variety of different problems to develop more sophisticated iterating and partitioning strategies. By posing the types of problems illustrated here, you can help your students develop the ability to iterate and partition in ways that might not have occurred to them naturally, without asking them to memorize algorithms that they might not be ready to make sense of at this point. In this way, you can *scaffold* their understanding of proportionality.

In everyday life, the term *scaffold* usually describes a structure erected around the outside of a building under construction for the purpose of supporting workers as they build. The key to the pedagogical meaning of *scaffold* is the idea of *support*—you scaffold instruction by supporting students' efforts without solving the problem for them or simplifying it so much that solving it becomes all but effortless.

ti p Teaching Tip

Scaffold students' progress as you offer them opportunities to engage in mathematical challenges that will facilitate their transition to more sophisticated levels of proportional reasoning.

It is often tempting to provide too much help when students struggle with ratio and proportion problems, thus removing their opportunities for genuine engagement with the mathematics. For example, consider the following problem:

Heart A beats 15 times in 8 seconds, and heart B beats 38 times in 20 seconds. Which heart is beating faster, A or B, or do they both beat at the same pace?

The discussion that follows presents two different dialogues between a teacher and a student working on the problem. The dialogues are based on an unpublished, small-scale study and reflect the general tone and substance of the interactions, although they are not direct transcripts.

Student: I don't know how to solve this problem. I'm stuck.

Teacher: How can you compare two heart rates?

Student: I don't know.

Teacher: Think of other rates you've heard of before. What are some rates you know of?

Student: Well ... there's miles per hour.

Teacher: Good. What makes that a rate?

Student: Because it has a *per*.

Teacher: Another way of saying that is because it's "per one." How many miles you travel in one hour. So how can you turn this into a rate?

Student: Find a "per one"?

Teacher: Good. So do you think it should be beats per minute or minutes per beat?

Student: Beats per minute.

Teacher: Okay, so divide to see how many beats per minute each heart will give you.

Reflect 3.2 asks you to evaluate the teacher's handling of the various "teachable moments" in this scenario.

Reflect 3.2

Consider the dialogue above in which the student struggles to determine which heart is beating faster.

a. Do you think the teacher provides the student with sufficiently rich problem-solving opportunities?

b. In what ways might you intervene differently with your own students?

Do you think the teacher helps the student too much? Are you nevertheless unsure about how you could manage the dialogue differently? Consider the following alternative scenario, in which the teacher scaffolds the student's thinking but deliberately avoids solving the problem for her:

Student: I don't know how to solve this problem. I'm stuck.

Teacher: What's the problem asking you to do?

Student: Figure out which heart is faster.

Teacher: Okay, so what does "faster" mean to you?

Student: Whichever heart beats quicker ... has more beats.

Teacher: Okay, ... so does that help you answer the question?

Student: Well, B gives 38 beats, but it takes more time—20 seconds instead of 8.

Teacher: Why does that matter?

Student: How many seconds it takes matters too. That's why I'm stuck.

Teacher: Ah, okay. So beats *and* seconds matter?

Student: Yeah.

Teacher: So you have A that gives 15 beats in 8 seconds, and B that gives 38 beats in 20 seconds. Can you figure out a way to compare those two?

Student: I can't really do it, because even though 38 is more than 15, 20 is also more than 8.

Teacher: Let me give you a different problem. Say that A gives 15 beats in 8 seconds, but B gives 20 beats in 16 seconds. Which heart beats faster?

Student: Hmmm... [*Starts to write*].

Teacher: I'll leave you to work on this for a while.

...

Teacher: So what did you figure out?

Student: Well, this one was pretty easy because if A beats 15 in 8 seconds, you can just multiply that by 2 and get 30 beats in 16 seconds. That's more than 20 beats in 16 seconds, so A has to be faster.

Teacher: Okay, so it looks like you multiplied A by 2. Why did you do that?

Student: Because then I have the same number of seconds.

Teacher: Why is that important?

> *Student*:   Because if the time is the same, then I can just see which heart had more beats in the same amount of time.
>
> *Teacher*:   So is there a way you could do that to solve the original problem?
>
> *Student*:   Make the time the same? I don't know, because the numbers don't work out very well.
>
> *Teacher*:   Why don't you try it out—see what you can come up with. I'll come back in a little while to see how you're doing.

Imagine what might have happened next: the student might have taken the 15:8 ratio and multiplied it by 2 to get 30:16. She might then have tried to compare 30:16 to 38:20. Suppose that she was still unable to tell which heart beats faster. She might then have realized that 20 seconds is 4 more than 16 seconds and that she could halve the 15:8 ratio to get 7.5:4. She might then have added 30 beats and 7.5 beats, and 16 seconds and 4 seconds, to obtain 37.5 beats in 20 seconds. Once she had determined that heart A gives 37.5 beats in 20 seconds and heart B gives 38 beats in the same amount of time, she could then conclude that heart B beats faster.

In this second scenario, the teacher allows the student to struggle with how to determine which heart beats faster. The student figures out that she has to take into account both seconds and beats in some way. At this stage in her development, it might not be clear to her that she can compare *either* the number of seconds for the same number of beats or the number of beats for the same number of seconds.

Students do not fully understand proportions until their thinking includes *reversibility*, which involves conceiving of a ratio in a way that allows for predicting with *both* quantities—not just one. An appropriate follow-up would be to provide problems in which it is easy to make the number of beats equal but difficult to make the number of seconds equal. This will help you determine whether the student realizes that he or she can compare *either* the number of beats when the time is the same *or* the time when the number of beats is the same.

The student in the second dialogue had the opportunity to develop a strategy based on halving and doubling to compare the two heart rates. This type of basic iterating and partitioning might be a necessary stage for the student before she is ready to understand why a strategy relying on a unit ratio would work. In follow-up problems, you can provide numbers that encourage the student to go beyond doubling and halving, perhaps taking thirds, fifths, or other fractions of the beats:second pairs. Ultimately, when the student develops facility in using a variety of "building-up" strategies, you can introduce problems with numbers that are relatively prime to encourage a unit ratio strategy. For instance, you can modify the heart problem as follows:

> Heart C beats 12 times in 17 seconds, and heart D beats 13 times in 18 seconds. Which heart is beating faster, C or D, or do they both beat at the same pace?

By allowing your students to struggle as they compare rates, to work on a variety of proportional-reasoning strategies, and to slowly develop an understanding of the need for a unit ratio strategy, you can help them build a flexible knowledge of ratios.

Shift 3—From composed-unit strategies to multiplicative comparisons

Although students may develop facility with proportional situations by iterating, partitioning, and using other building-up strategies with composed units, they also need to be able to compare quantities multiplicatively, using a crucial part of Essential Understanding 2 related to ratios: "A ratio is a multiplicative comparison of two quantities." Mastering this important skill allows students to make another shift toward proportional reasoning.

This shift may take time, since many students find working with composed units more natural than forming multiplicative comparisons. For instance, the middle school students who worked with the problem of the two interlocking gears solved the following problem in the same context:

> If Gear A has 8 teeth and gear B has 12 teeth, and gear A turns 96 times, how many times will gear B turn?

The students' solution process may seem cumbersome. Dani explained her solution as follows: "We know that A turns 3 times when B turns twice. So we can take 3 : 2 and repeat it. 3 : 2, 6 : 4, 12 : 8, 24 : 16, 48 : 32, 96 : 64. So B turned 64 times." Although simply multiplying 96 by $^2/_3$ would be much faster, Dani probably had not yet thought of gear B as turning $^2/_3$ as many times as gear A. That is, she had not compared the rotations of gear A and gear B multiplicatively.

Even though Dani's method of iterating may seem unnecessarily time-consuming, it could be the very process that she needs to go through—perhaps many times—before she feels comfortable moving on to other strategies. With this in mind, consider allowing your students to progress at their own rates. Instead of providing more efficient strategies up front, consider posing problems whose solutions would make a student's building-up strategy inconvenient.

Shift 3

Students need to make a transition from using only composed-unit strategies to making and using multiplicative comparisons as well.

Essential ←
Understanding 2

A ratio is a multiplicative comparison of two quantities, or it is a joining of two quantities into a composed unit.

For instance, a problem with large numbers could prompt students to shift to a different strategy if iterating is too much trouble. A good problem to help Dani make the shift to multiplicative comparisons might be the following:

> Gear A has 8 teeth, and gear B has 12 teeth. If gear A turns 1,257 times, how many times will gear B turn?

Simply teaching Dani to multiply 96 rotations by $2/3$ might have allowed her to solve this problem and others very similar to it. However, the fact that Dani went through the tedious process of iterating the $3:2$ ratio so many times could also mean that she was not ready to make sense of a multiplication strategy or to form a multiplicative comparison.

Progressing through these shifts in reasoning can be intellectually difficult for students; the transitions take time and effort. However, the goal is to help students develop the ability to reason proportionally and ultimately solve a variety of problems, both standard and nonstandard. Unfortunately, early reliance on any strategy or algorithm that you offer or impose can allow your students to avoid the difficult work involved in developing proportional reasoning.

Instead, you can pose problems like the one about the two gears, with one gear now making 1257 turns, as well as other problems that encourage the formation of multiplicative comparisons in other ways. Consider, for example, the following new problem involving the interlocking gears:

> Gear A has 8 teeth, and gear B has 12 teeth. Suppose that you needed to replace gear A with a new gear that would make gear B turn twice as fast as it did before. How many teeth would the new gear A have to have? What if you wanted gear B to turn twice as slowly as it did before? How many teeth would the new gear A need to have in this case?

Reflect 3.3 invites you to think about what your students might gain from solving this problem.

Teaching Tip

Encourage students to develop their own appropriate strategies, and only judiciously introduce strategies such as the formation of a multiplicative comparison or the use of multiplication.

Reflect 3.3

Consider the problem involving a new gear A that makes gear B turn twice as fast or twice as slowly as before. How could you use this problem to encourage your students to form multiplicative comparisons?

This problem encourages a multiplicative comparison because it is helpful to know how much of a rotation gear B makes when gear A turns once. When gear A has 8 teeth, gear B turns $8/12$, or $2/3$, of a rotation. Doubling the number of teeth on gear A to 16 teeth will mean that gear B will turn $^{16}/_{12}$, or $^4/_3$, rotations when gear A turns once. Halving the number of teeth on gear A will mean that gear B will turn $^1/_3$ of a rotation when gear A turns once.

A related problem that you could pose to students follows:

Gear A and gear B turn together. Gear A has 6 teeth, and in a period of time, gear B turns $^1/_4$ as many revolutions as gear A. How many teeth does gear B have?

Once students can solve these sorts of problems and have started to think about one quantity as being twice as great as another, or even $^1/_2$ or $^1/_4$ as great as another, you can help them connect multiplicative comparisons with composed units, as highlighted in Essential Understanding 7. A flexible understanding of ratios and proportions will include the knowledge that a ratio such as "3 turns for every 2 turns" means that the number of rotations for gear A is $^3/_2$ as many as the number of rotations for gear B.

By giving your students multiple problems at times when they are ready to tackle them, you can help them develop an understanding of building-up strategies, multiplicative comparisons, and the connections between them. In addition, by giving students opportunities to think about how their ways of solving a problem might generalize to an entire class of problems, you can help them develop a flexible, powerful set of ideas about ratios and proportions.

Once students have had the opportunity to solve proportion problems with the strategies discussed above, you might consider introducing an algorithm as a standard way to solve the problems. If students already possess a strong understanding of proportional situations, then they will be poised to make sense of an algorithm and compare it meaningfully with their own ways of solving problems. When it comes to introducing algorithms, the most important factor is your judgment about students' readiness.

Shift 4—From iterating a composed unit to creating many equivalent ratios

The final important transition addressed in this chapter is the shift from being able to iterate a composed unit, like Dani did, to creating infinitely many equivalent ratios. It is a mistake to assume that students who can iterate or partition a composed unit have a full understanding of ratios and rates. Students can be capable of doubling and halving a composed unit without understanding that it is possible to multiply a ratio by *any* real number while maintaining the same relationship.

One way to help students make the transition to developing equivalent ratios that do not depend on easy multiples is to pose

Essential ← Understanding 7

Proportional reasoning is complex and involves understanding that—

- *equivalent ratios can be created by iterating and/ or partitioning a composed unit;*
- *if one quantity in a ratio is multiplied or divided by a particular factor, then the other quantity must be multiplied or divided by the same factor to maintain the proportional relationship; and*
- *the two types of ratios—composed units and multiplicative comparisons—are related.*

Shift 4

Students need to make a transition from developing a few "easy" equivalent ratios to creating a set of infinitely many equivalent ratios.

problems that encourage them to consider equivalent ratios with "messy" numbers. For example, consider the Pasta Sauce problem:

> Zadora sells pasta sauce and charges $3.00 for a 7-ounce jar or $16.00 for two jars that hold a total of $37\frac{1}{3}$ ounces. Is buying a 7-ounce jar a better deal than buying two jars that hold $37\frac{1}{3}$ ounces? How do you know?

This type of problem may encourage students to develop unit ratio strategies, but you can also redirect students' attention back to the two original ratios. Do these ratios represent the same cost per ounce? If so, how can this be, since none of the numbers is a multiple of any other? You can then lead students in a discussion of what types of ratios can be equivalent to others, ultimately encouraging the development of the idea of a rate as a set of infinitely many equivalent ratios, as reflected in Essential Understanding 8.

Alternatively, you could present your students with a table of values such as that in figure 3.4, which shows corresponding weights (in pounds) of objects on Earth and on another planet. You might ask, "Given each pair of weights of in the table, how can you tell whether every weight B that was determined 'on another planet' was determined on the *same* other planet?" You could go on to ask, "In any new pair of weights A and B that I come up with, how could you tell that weight B was determined on this same planet?"

Essential Understanding 8

A rate is a set of infinitely many equivalent ratios.

Teaching Tip

Focus on generalizing and justifying to encourage students to—
- *make connections between building-up strategies and multiplicative comparisons;*
- *appreciate the relationships between informal strategies and formal algorithms; and*
- *develop an understanding of rate as a set of infinitely many equivalent ratios.*

	Weight A on Earth (lbs.)	Weight B on Another Planet (lbs.)
Object 1	120	45
Object 2	27	$10\frac{1}{8}$
Object 3	42	$15\frac{3}{4}$
Object 4	16	6
Object 5	$\frac{1}{10}$	$\frac{9}{240}$

Fig. 3.4. A table showing corresponding weights A and B of objects on Earth and on another planet

This problem and the Pasta Sauce problem, although very different on the surface, have several things in common. First, both emphasize quantities and quantitative relationships. Second, both encourage students to explain their reasoning, make generalizations, or provide a justification. These are important features of problems that help students make the fourth shift in their thinking.

The Pasta Sauce problem encourages students to think about whether the cost per ounce of the 7-ounce jar is the same as that of the two jars that together hold $37\frac{1}{3}$ ounces. Both are representations of the same rate ($2\frac{1}{3}$ ounces per dollar or about 43 cents per ounce), and once students have determined this, you can ask them to think about what is similar in the two representations. Likewise, working with the weight table encourages students to think about what is the same for all of the pairs and ultimately express that relationship as $B = \frac{3}{8}A$, $A = \frac{8}{3}B$, or in some other way. By generalizing from different instantiations of the same relationship, students can gain facility in expressing relationships in verbal and algebraic descriptions.

You can also emphasize the process of generalizing by asking your students to—

- describe what is similar in different representations;

- think about whether a pattern that they noticed will extend to different types of numbers;

- describe situations or cases in which a pattern or relationship would not apply; and

- express an observed pattern or relationship in general terms.

The students whose work with the two interlocking gears was discussed above also worked with speed situations, including the situation involving the clown and the frog described in chapters 1 and 2. Their teacher asked them to think about what, if anything, was the same about the speed problems and the gear problems. The following dialogue is an example of the type of conversation that can occur when teachers encourage generalizing:

Larissa: Okay. We always have two things. Either there's ... there's either seconds and centimeters, or rotations and ... rotations.

Jamie: And it's gonna be a straight line.

Teacher: Why would it be a straight line?

Larissa: Because all of them are the same relationship.

Jamie: Because it's consistent, and consistent also means, like, keep going. And linear means like keep –

Timothy: No, it won't be.

Jamie: It will, because they both keep going at the same pace.

Teacher: So what does that mean, "keep going at the same pace"? Let's think back to the gears. What did the "same pace" mean for the gears?

Mandy: Like with the $\frac{2}{3}$ gear relationship, Gear B always turned $\frac{2}{3}$ as much as gear A. Every time you spun it, that was consistent.

Teacher:	So why is that like speed?
Larissa:	It would be the same as if the clown walked $2/3$ of a centimeter per second. If his speed was $2/3$, it's the same thing as the gears. Every second he walks, he goes $2/3$ of a centimeter no matter what. It is a steady pace.
Timothy:	Both of them have to have the same steady pace, and if the pace always remains steady, then it will be a line.
Teacher:	Do you think that is just for gears and speed, or could you have other things that make a line too?
Larissa:	You could have other things—
Timothy:	You could basically have anything that would make a line, as long as the pace is steady, like $2/3$ of something per something, like a car driving.

By encouraging the students to think about what made data linear for both the speed and gear situations, the teacher shifted the classroom focus away from the production of a specific rule to the mathematical process of generalizing. The students created a number of different algebraic representations in various forms, all of which made sense to them, given their understanding of the nature of speed and gear rotations. These experiences allowed the teacher to lead discussions about why different algebraic forms of the same relationship are mathematically equivalent.

By the time the preceding conversation occurred, the students had already created algebraic rules such as $B = 2/3A$. The formalization of a relationship or a pattern is only part of a student's mathematical journey; students also need opportunities to explain why their rules makes sense and to think about the origin of algebraic rules.

By focusing on justification—both their own and their peers'— students can examine their ideas about equivalent ratios, exploring why many different ratios can all represent the same relationship. These justifying and generalizing actions support the development of equivalent ratios and eventually lead to the idea of rate. In addition, an environment that encourages justification will allow students to make judgments about the strategies and explanations of their classmates, a process that provides additional learning opportunities.

This chapter's discussion of students' learning of proportional reasoning has consistently highlighted an important curricular and teaching emphasis. The sample problems and the dialogues accompanying them have all stressed the need to offer students ratio and proportion situations that they can make sense of in the context of real-world quantities. By supporting their reasoning about quantitative relationships in everyday situations like that involving gear ratios, students can make sense of an idea like "steady rotations" and connect that idea with a constant ratio. In addition, the quantitative relationships can support the many ways in which students think about ratio, including doubling and halving, using other iterating and partitioning strategies, building up to equivalent ratios, or using unit ratio strategies.

However, it is important to be aware that students may still be prone to focus solely on number patterns—especially when the numbers are presented in tabular form. Once students begin thinking about numbers and number patterns instead of the quantities that they represent, developing appropriate generalizations about ratio and rate may be harder for them—not to mention the even greater challenge of providing mathematically sound justifications.

As a teacher, however, you can play an important role in helping your students focus on quantities and the language of quantitative relationships. One way to do so is to incorporate the language of quantities into the classroom discussion, as the teacher did in the dialogue about the quantitative relationships in the gear and speed situations. For instance, if you had a student who examined the table in figure 3.2, which shows rotation pairs for gears A and B, and then described the pattern as "B divided by A is always $2/3$," you could ask her to think about whether that would mean that all of the data pairs came from the same two gears. Or if you had a student who was working in the context of the Pasta Sauce problem and described a pattern such as "each time x goes up by 7, y goes up by 3," you could respond by asking him to explain whether that would mean that each jar of pasta sauce costs the same amount, or if some are more expensive than others. If we encourage students to build ratios from relationships between quantities that make sense to them, they will have a better chance of forming representations that are grounded in their ways of making sense of the world.

tip Teaching Tip

Refocus students' attention on quantities and quantitative relationships to emphasize the meaning of constant ratios.

The Role of Informal Assessment

One way to assess students' understanding is by pushing them to explain their thinking as they solve problems like the ones discussed above. Students' responses to those problems can reveal a great deal about their understanding of ratio situations. For instance, Dani's solution to the Connected Gears problem revealed that she was comparing quantities additively. Her response to a follow-up problem that called on her to find the number of rotations for gear B when gear A turned 96 times suggested that Dani needed to iterate a composed unit repeatedly because she had not yet reached the stage of forming a multiplicative comparison. Even though her solution was correct, Dani's explanation of her thinking revealed important information about her level of understanding—the kind of information that you might not get from your students through a quiz or test problem.

Students might be able to solve a problem correctly, but their justifications can show you *how* they are thinking about the problem. Consider, for instance, the work of students on a task similar to the "head start" problem discussed in chapter 2 (see p. 52). Figure 3.5 shows the particular problem that the students were considering—the Clown's Journey problem. Notice that the –5 in the first row of the table means that the character was 5 centimeters behind his house after 2 seconds of the journey. In contrast, the data in the second row mean that the clown was 20 centimeters in front of his house after 12 seconds.

Clown's Journey Problem

The following table represents the clown's location from home, and his time:

Location (cm)	Elapsed Time (sec)
–5	2
20	12
40	20
52.5	25
140	60

a. Did the clown walk at the same speed, or did he speed up or slow down? How can you tell?

b. Describe the journey that the clown made that generated these pairs.

Fig. 3.5. The Clown's Journey problem

Julie correctly observed that the clown walked 2.5 centimeters per second, and that he had started his journey 10 centimeters "behind his house" (that is, 10 centimeters measured from his house in the opposite direction from that in which he was traveling). She decided that he had walked the same speed throughout his entire journey. However, when asked to justify her solution, Julie ran into difficulties:

Julie: I was finding out the gaps between all the numbers, like –5 and 20, and 2 and 12, and so on, for both sides. And when I got both, I divided 25 by 10 and 20 by 8 and 12.5 by 5 and 87.5 by 35, and it all gave me 2.5, which was his speed.

Teacher: How did you know that 2.5 was the clown's speed?

Julie: Well, I just guessed.

Teacher: How did you make that guess?

Julie: Because that's what she, that's what Larissa did yesterday.

When pressed, Julie could not explain why dividing the differences of the centimeters by the differences of the seconds made sense. Although her written work was correct, Julie's verbal justification revealed that she did not necessarily recognize a constant rate in the situation; she had only managed to memorize a procedure that she apparently did not connect with her understanding of ratios.

This exchange highlights the importance of asking students to explain their thinking and provide justifications for their reasoning. The teacher's follow-up question, "How did you know that 2.5 was the clown's speed?" demonstrates the need to push students beyond simply describing *what* they did to solve the problem. Larissa was subsequently able to explain why Julie's procedure made sense: "If he can go 20 centimeters in 8 seconds, to find out how many centimeters he can go in 1 second, you have to divide by 8 because there's a total of 8 seconds. And then if you divide 20 by 8 you'll get 2.5, which is ... that's how far he went in 1 second."

Multiple problem types

Although asking students to explain their reasoning and provide justifications can be an excellent way to determine their level of understanding, these classroom conversations are unlikely to be fruitful unless the tasks presented are genuine problems instead of exercises. Figure 3.6 shows an example of an exercise, which Reflect 3.4 encourages you to compare and contrast with a genuine problem.

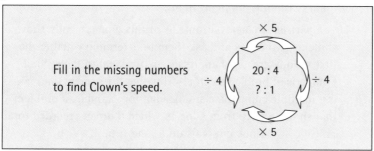

Fig. 3.6. An example of an "exercise"

The task in the figure is an exercise rather than a problem for most students for several reasons. First, it does not require students

Reflect 3.4

Would the task in figure 3.6 be a genuine problem for your students? Explain. If so, how could you change it into an exercise? If not, how could you change it into a genuine problem?

to figure out something new on their own. Instead, it gives them the solution method pictorially. Second, although it appears to involve students in learning about ratios, it does not require them to create ratios to solve the problem. Instead, it merely asks them to follow the directions, either dividing 20 by 4 or multiplying 1 by 5, to fill in the missing number. In contrast, a genuine ratio problem would require students to form a ratio, without giving a recipe for doing so.

The distinction between a problem and an exercise can be a useful one for you to consider when making decisions about what opportunities to provide for your students. The problems presented previously in this chapter, such as the Connected Gears problem, are genuine in the sense that they—

- provide opportunities for students to construct ratios;
- ask students to tackle a novel situation; and
- give students room to determine solutions on their own.

Although it is important to provide students with opportunities to strengthen their skills, exercises like the one shown in figure 3.6 do not focus on *ratio* skills; they simply require students to practice whole-number multiplication or division skills.

You may want to give your students problems of different types to assess their proportional reasoning abilities and help them develop new understanding. The previous discussion of shifts in students' thinking included examples of some types, and the discussion that follows adds examples of other types, illustrating five major types of proportional reasoning problems in all:

1. *Comparison problems.* Problems of this type typically show students two ratios and ask them to determine whether the first ratio is greater than, less than, or equal to the second. Comparison problems can also involve the students in making multiple comparisons. Consider, for example, a problem that shows a page from a log in which a driver recorded total mileage at various intervals on a long trip:

   After 2, 5, 7, and 8 hours of driving, the driver recorded the distance as 130 miles, 325 miles, 445 miles, and 510 miles, respectively. Was the driver traveling at a constant speed throughout the trip, or did he speed up and slow down?

Several of the problems previously discussed are examples of comparison problems, including the problems about heartbeats and the weights of objects, and some of the speed problems.

2. *Transformation problems.* Problems of this type typically give a ratio or two equivalent ratios and ask students either to change one or more quantities to change the ratio relationship or to determine how a given change in one or more quantities changes the relationship. For instance, consider the following speed problem:

During a morning journey, Clown and Frog walked at the same speed, although Clown traveled more distance and took more time than Frog. In the afternoon, Clown and Frog took a second journey. Clown traveled twice as much distance as he had in the morning but in the same amount of time. Frog traveled the same distance as he had in the morning but in half the time. Did Clown walk faster, slower, or the same speed as Frog in the afternoon?

In this problem, students are asked to consider the effect that doubling one quantity has on a particular ratio, compared with halving the other quantity.

3. *Mean value problems.* Mean value problems present a scenario with an underlying structure of the form

$$\frac{A}{x} = \frac{x}{B}$$

and call on students to find the value of x so that the relationship will hold. An example follows:

Gear A has 48 teeth, and gear C has 12 teeth. How many teeth should gear B have so that the ratio of revolutions of gear A to gear B is the same as the ratio of revolutions from gear B to gear C?

4. *Part-part-whole and containment problems.* Problems in this category express a set in terms of two or more subsets. For instance, students might be shown two pictures of lemonade—one made from 8 cups of water and 4 cups of lemon concentrate, and another consisting of 10 cups of water and 6 cups of lemon concentrate—and be asked which lemonade mixture will taste stronger. Part-part-whole problems span many levels of difficulty depending on their features. For example, consider the following two problems from Kaput and Maxwell-West (1994, p. 246):

a. To make Italian dressing, you need 4 parts vinegar for 9 parts oil. How much oil do you need for 828 ounces of vinegar?

b. A large restaurant sets tables by putting 7 pieces of silverware and 4 pieces of china on each placemat. If it used 392 pieces of silverware in its table settings last night, how many pieces of china did it use?

Reflect 3.5 asks you to consider how your students might respond to these problems.

Reflect 3.5

Which of these two problems do you think your students would find more difficult to solve? Why?

Researchers found that the oil and vinegar problem was much harder for students than the placemat problem (Kaput and Maxwell-West 1994). They conjectured that the placemat problem was easier for students because of their perception of "containment" in the situation. The placemats held the parts—namely, the silverware and the china—and these items were well identified and distinct. The fact that the placemat held the two types of items together seemed to support a build-up strategy. Even though the oil and vinegar problem also had containment, the parts seemed ambiguous, and they lacked easily imagined containers. When the students imagined the oil and vinegar as mixed, these ingredients seemed to lose their separate identities, and the blending appeared to create an additional challenge to keeping the quantities conceptually separate.

5. *Geometric similarity and scaling.* Problems of this type, which involve similarity, scaling, stretching, or shrinking, are the most difficult for students to recognize as proportional (Kaput and Maxwell-West 1994). Figure 3.7 presents a problem of this type. One reason that such problems are so challenging may be that students cannot usually solve them easily by iterating or partitioning a composed unit. For example, to solve the problem in the figure, you cannot easily cut and paste copies of the smaller rectangle to fit in the larger. Instead, the growth from the smaller to the larger rectangle results from simultaneously increasing, stretching, or pulling both dimensions in a coordinated manner.

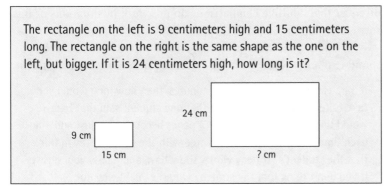

The rectangle on the left is 9 centimeters high and 15 centimeters long. The rectangle on the right is the same shape as the one on the left, but bigger. If it is 24 centimeters high, how long is it?

Fig. 3.7. A problem involving similarity

Assessing levels of proportional reasoning

This chapter has discussed some of the shifts that students make as they become more adept at reasoning proportionally. It has also presented problems designed to help students make these shifts. This final section elaborates a few ways to assess the type of reasoning in which students may engage—whether they are reasoning additively or with ratios, whether they are reasoning with composed units or multiplicative comparisons, and whether or not they understand unit ratios.

Assessing whether students are reasoning additively or with ratios

Problems such as the Connected Gears problem provide opportunities for students to form ratios. However, even when students are able to construct ratios, they may revert to additive reasoning if the differences between the quantities given in a problem are relatively small. You can use problems such as the following to identify this tendency in your students:

> Suppose that you have two interlocking gears—a big gear and a small gear. When the small gear turns 12 times, the big gear turns 9 times. If the small gear turns 13 times, how many times will the big gear turn?

This problem is a missing-value problem in which the differences between the quantities are small. A possible response indicating additive reasoning is that the big gear will turn 10 times. If your students are working physically with gears, you can invite them to test their hypothesis by turning the gears and counting the rotations. Once they discover that the big gear does not quite turn 10 times, you can ask them to think about why that might be the case. Testing hypotheses in this way gives students opportunities to discover that additive comparisons do not work in situations of this sort, potentially prompting them to adopt a new approach.

Consider a different problem—one that invites students to respond explicitly to the additive reasoning of a hypothetical student:

> If Sara can read 12 pages in 15 minutes, then how long would she take to read 13 pages? Suppose that one student said that Sara would take 16 minutes to read 13 pages because "you just add 1 on each time." Do you agree or disagree with the student? If you think that the student's strategy works, show how, and justify your answer. If you don't think that the strategy works, explain why not.

A problem like this can elicit evidence of your students' tendency to use additive reasoning even if other problems do not, because it poses a common way of thinking that students must either accept or reject. By allowing students to engage in a group discussion over whether the hypothetical student's approach makes sense, you can judge how robust their reasoning with ratios is and how strong their inclination is to use additive comparisons.

Presenting ideas as originating with hypothetical students can be a valuable way of eliciting students' thinking. Because the proposed idea purportedly comes from another student rather than from you—the teacher—the idea will not carry your authority, and your students will be less likely to agree with it simply because they want to agree with you. You can pose both correct and incorrect strategies as the ideas of hypothetical students.

Assessing students' abilities to reason with composed units or multiplicative comparisons

A good way to prompt students to form multiplicative comparisons is to have them explore tables of data or solve prediction problems with large numbers, such as the gear problems on page 70. Another way to assess a student's thinking is to present a problem that calls on him or her to draw and use a picture in the explanation of a solution. Consider the following problem:

> Frog walks 5 centimeters in 4 seconds. Clown walks 15 centimeters in 12 seconds. Does one character walk faster than the other, or are the two characters walking equally fast? Draw a picture to explain your answer.

Larissa, one student who was solving this problem, created the drawing in figure 3.8. The top line represents Frog's journey: the numbers on the line represent the centimeters, and the numbers in the boxes represent the seconds. Frog's journey continued for 4 seconds, in which time he traveled 5 centimeters. Clown's journey,

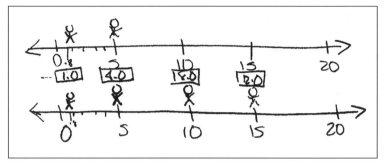

Fig. 3.8. A student's picture showing that Frog and Clown traveled at the same speed (from Ellis [2007], p. 219)

represented by the bottom number line, continued for 12 seconds, in which time he traveled 15 centimeters.

Larissa concluded that the characters walked the same speed because she could think of Clown's journey as Frog's journey repeated:

> When they're at 5, both of them are at 4.0 seconds. But since the frog stops, he's finished.... But the clown keeps going, and from 0 to 5, it jumped 4 seconds.... From 5 to 10, it also jumped 5 centimeters and 4 seconds. And from 10 to 15, it jumped 5 centimeters and also 4, um, seconds. So the proportion stays the same throughout the thing, even though the frog stopped.

Larissa's explanation, in combination with her drawing, demonstrates that she is thinking of a composed unit (5 cm : 4 sec). This response could be an indication that she needs to solve more problems like the ones shown earlier in the chapter to encourage the formation and use of multiplicative comparisons, in addition to the use of composed units.

Assessing students' understanding of unit ratios

Essential Understanding 9 states that several informal ways of reasoning can be generalized into algorithms for solving proportion problems. For students to grasp this essential understanding, it is critically important for them to develop a deep understanding of unit ratios, as chapter 1 suggests. They can then use this understanding to develop an alternative to the cross-multiplication algorithm—a different algorithm that is generalizable and grounded in sense making.

Furthermore, a component of understanding unit ratios is being able to reinterpret ratios as quotients, as indicated in Essential Understanding 5. To help you assess your students' understanding of the important relationship between unit ratios and division, you can give them problems that invite them to draw pictures, such as the following:

Essential ⬅
Understanding 9

Several ways of reasoning, all grounded in sense making, can be generalized into algorithms for solving proportion problems.

Essential ⬅
Understanding 5

Ratios can be meaningfully reinterpreted as quotients.

Suppose that 15 hoagies are to be shared to feed 12 people. To decide how to share the hoagies, a student divides 12 by 15 to get 0.8 people per hoagie. Does this student's work give a good way to share the hoagies? Draw a picture to support your answer.

A different way of using pictures to help you assess this understanding is to ask your students to make sense of given pictures to solve problems. Consider the problem in figure 3.9, which includes a picture.

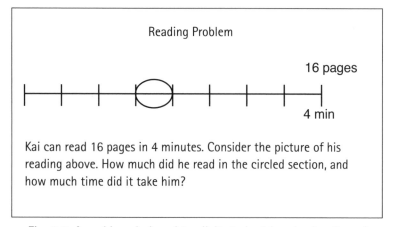

Fig. 3.9. A problem designed to elicit students' understanding of division and unit ratios

Students who tackle the problem without recognizing a strong connection between division and partitioning, or without fully understanding unit ratios, may incorrectly divide the number of pages (16) by the number of minutes (4) instead of by the number of partitioned groups (8) yielding an incorrect response of 4 pages in 1 minute. If this happens, you could follow up by asking students to show their answer in the drawing and to fill in the number of minutes and pages that go with the other tick marks in the diagram. By doing so, the students are likely to notice that something is not right. For example, if a student treats each segment as representing 4 pages in 1 minute, and labels the tick marks from left to right, he or she will reach 16 pages in 4 minutes much too soon—just halfway through the picture. If students are still stuck, you might interpret their confusion as a sign that you need to take a step back and help them develop their understanding of division and partitioning by building on their natural halving strategies.

Conclusion

Informal and formal assessment strategies that ask students to draw their own pictures, explain their reasoning, provide justifications for their answers, and interpret other people's pictures, strategies, and solutions can provide new insight into students' levels of proportional reasoning. Consider providing students with a variety of problems to assess their understanding of the same idea in different ways. As this chapter has shown, students may be able to solve problems correctly, yet not really understand the situations at hand or the solutions that they have given. Asking them to provide justifications, drawings, or solutions to different problems can reveal that their understanding is not as strong as their performances initially seem to suggest. Recall Bonita's work from chapter 1. Although Bonita could use the cross-multiplication algorithm to solve a proportion problem correctly, her subsequent work revealed a number of significant gaps in her understanding.

Be wary of overestimating students' understanding on the basis of their ability to use an algorithm correctly. A better way to gauge students' proportional reasoning is to provide problems that represent a variety of types and go beyond the typical missing-value problems. By posing problems of assorted types and forms, you will be able to determine with greater accuracy how your students are reasoning.

References

Barnett-Clarke, Carne, William Fisher, Rick Marks, and Sharon Ross. *Developing Essential Understanding of Rational Numbers for Teaching Mathematics in Grades 3–5*. Essential Understanding Series. Reston, Va.: National Council of Teachers of Mathematics, forthcoming.

Clark, Faye B., and Constance Kamii. "Identification of Multiplicative Thinking in Children in Grades 1–5." *Journal for Research in Mathematics Education* 27 (January 1996): 41–51.

Clark, Matthew R., Sarah B. Berenson, and Laurie O. Cavey. "A Comparison of Ratios and Fractions and Their Roles as Tools in Proportional Reasoning." *Journal of Mathematical Behavior* 22 (August 2003): 297–317.

Ellis, Amy. "Connections between Generalizing and Justifying: Students' Reasoning with Linear Relationships." *Journal for Research in Mathematics Education* 38 (May 2007): 194–229.

Harel, Guershon, Merlyn Behr, Richard Lesh, and Thomas Post. "Invariance of Ratio: The Case of Children's Anticipatory Scheme for Constancy of Taste." *Journal for Research in Mathematics Education* 25 (July 1994): 324–45.

Kaput, James, and Mary Maxwell-West. "Missing-Value Proportional Reasoning Problems: Factors Affecting Informal Reasoning Patterns." In *The Development of Multiplicative Reasoning in the Learning of Mathematics*, edited by Guershon Harel and Jere Confrey, pp. 235–87. Albany, N.Y.: State University of New York Press, 1994.

Karplus, Robert, Steven Pulos, and Elizabeth Stage. "Early Adolescents' Proportional Reasoning on Rate Problems." *Educational Studies in Mathematics* 14 (August 1983): 219–33.

Lamon, Susan J. *Teaching Fractions and Ratios for Understanding: Essential Content Knowledge and Instructional Strategies for Teachers*. 1st ed. Mahwah, N.J.: Lawrence Erlbaum Associates, 1999.

Lehrer, Richard. "Developing Understanding of Measurement." In *A Research Companion to "Principles and Standards for School Mathematics,"* edited by Jeremy Kilpatrick, W. Gary Martin, and Deborah Schifter, pp. 179–92. Reston, Va.: National Council of Teachers of Mathematics, 2003.

Lesh, Richard, Thomas Post, and Merlyn Behr. "Proportional Reasoning." In *Number Concepts and Operations in the Middle Grades*, edited by James Hiebert and Merlyn Behr, pp. 93–118. Reston, Va.: National Council of Teachers of Mathematics, 1988.

Lobato, Joanne. "When Students Don't Apply the Knowledge
     You Think They Have, Rethink Your Assumptions about
     Transfer." In *Making the Connection: Research and Teaching in
     Undergraduate Mathematics*, edited by Chris Rasmussen and
     Marilyn Carlson, pp. 287–302. Washington, D.C.: Mathematical
     Association of America, 2008.

Lobato, Joanne, and Eva Thanheiser. "Developing Understanding of
     Ratio as Measure as a Foundation for Slope." In *Making Sense
     of Fractions, Ratios, and Proportions*, 2002 Yearbook of the
     National Council of Teachers of Mathematics (NCTM), edited by
     Bonnie Litwiller, pp. 162–75. Reston, Va.: NCTM, 2002.

National Council of Teachers of Mathematics (NCTM). *Curriculum
     Focal Points for Prekindergarten through Grade 8 Mathematics*:
     A Quest for Coherence. Reston, Va.: NCTM, 2006.

———. *Principles and Standards for School Mathematics*. Reston, Va.:
     NCTM, 2000.

———. *Focus in High School Mathematics: Reasoning and Sense
     Making*. Reston, Va.: NCTM, 2009.

Roschelle, Jeremy, and James Kaput. "SimCalc MathWorlds for
     the Mathematics of Change." *Communications of the ACM* 39
     (August 1996): 97–99.

Simon, Martin A., and Glendon W. Blume. "Mathematical Modeling
     as a Component of Understanding Ratio-as-Measure: A
     Study of Prospective Elementary Teachers." *The Journal of
     Mathematical Behavior* 13 (June 1994): 183–97.

Steffe, Leslie. "Children's Multiplying Schemes." In *The Development
     of Multiplicative Reasoning in the Learning of Mathematics*,
     edited by Guershon Harel and Jere Confrey, pp. 3–40. Albany,
     N.Y.: State University of New York Press, 1994.

Thompson, Patrick W. "The Development of the Concept of Speed
     and Its Relationship to Concepts of Rate." *In The Development
     of Multiplicative Reasoning in the Learning of Mathematics*,
     edited by Guershon Harel and Jere Confrey, pp. 181–234.
     Albany, N.Y.: State University of New York Press, 1994.

Thompson, Patrick W., and Luis Saldanha. "Fractions and
     Multiplicative Reasoning." In *A Research Companion to
     "Principles and Standards for School Mathematics,"* edited
     by Jeremy Kilpatrick, W. Gary Martin, and Deborah Schifter,
     pp. 95–114. Reston, Va.: National Council of Teachers of
     Mathematics, 2003.

Titles in the Essential Understandings Series

The Essential Understanding Series gives teachers the deep understanding that they need to teach challenging topics in mathematics. Students encounter such topics across the pre-K–grade 12 curriculum, and teachers who understand the big ideas related to each topic can give maximum support as students develop their own understanding and make connections among important ideas.

Developing Essential Understanding of–
  Number and Numeration for Teaching Mathematics in Prekindergarten–Grade 2
  ISBN 978-0-87353-629-5   Stock No. 13492

  Addition and Subtraction for Teaching Mathematics in Prekindergarten–Grade 2
  ISBN 978-0-87353-664-6   Stock No. 13792

  Rational Numbers for Teaching Mathematics in Grades 3–5
  ISBN 978-0-87353-630-1   Stock No. 13493

  Algebraic Thinking for Teaching Mathematics in Grades 3–5
  ISBN 978-0-87353-668-4   Stock No. 13796

  Multiplication and Division for Teaching Mathematics in Grades 3–5
  ISBN 978-0-87353-667-7   Stock No. 13795

  Ratios, Proportions, and Proportional Reasoning for Teaching Mathematics in Grades 6–8
  ISBN 978-0-87353-622-6   Stock No. 13482

  Functions for Teaching Mathematics in Grades 9–12
  ISBN 978-0-87353-623-3   Stock No. 13483

Coming in Fall 2011:

Developing Essential Understanding of–
  Expressions, Equations, and Functions for Teaching Mathematics in Grades 6–8

  Mathematical Reasoning for Teaching Mathematics in Prekindergarten–Grade 8

Coming in 2012:

Developing Essential Understanding of–
  Geometry for Teaching Mathematics in Prekindergarten–Grade 2

  Geometry for Teaching Mathematics in Grades 3–5

  Geometry for Teaching Mathematics in Grades 6–8

  Geometry for Teaching Mathematics in Grades 9–12

  Reasoning and Proof for Teaching Mathematics in Grades 9–12

  Data for Teaching Mathematics in Grades 6–8

  Statistics for Teaching Mathematics in Grades 9–12

Visit www.nctm.org/catalog for details and ordering information.